To Dad

May this bring
you a few
CHUCKLES.

love

Sue & Phil

Xmas 1983.

☆ ☆ ☆ ☆ ☆

A FUNNY THING HAPPENED ON THE WAY TO THE WHITE HOUSE

A FUNNY THING HAPPENED ON THE WAY TO THE WHITE HOUSE

DAVID E. JOHNSON
JOHNNY R. JOHNSON

Beaufort Books, Inc. ● New York/ Toronto

Library of Congress Cataloging in Publication Data
Johnson, David E.
   A funny thing happened on the way to the White House.

   Bibliography: p.
   1. Presidents—United States—Anecdotes, facetiae, satire, etc.
I. Johnson, Johnny Ray. II. Title.
E176.1.J63   1983   973'.09'92   83-7085
ISBN 0-8253-0150-5

Chapter 8 reprinted courtesy of Historical Times, Inc., publishers of *American History Illustrated.*

Published in the United States by Beaufort Books, Inc., New York.
Published simultaneously in Canada by General Publishing Co. Limited

Designer: Cynthia Basil
Printed in the U.S.A.   First Edition
                    10 9 8 7 6 5 4 3 2 1

CONTENTS

★ ★ ★ ★ ★

A FUNNY THING HAPPENED ON THE WAY TO THE WHITE HOUSE

★ ★ ★ 1 ★ ★ ★
PRESIDENTIAL
POLITICS

"We do not believe that the American people will knowingly elect to the presidency a coarse debauchee who would bring his harlots with him to Washington and hire lodgings for them convenient to the White House."

—*New York Sun* description of Grover Cleveland

American presidential politics have many notable traditions, but probably none is so time honored or so ubiquitous as the slinging of mud.

As a vice-presidential candidate in 1952, Richard Nixon wasn't inventing a new ploy when he labeled the men who exposed his secret slush fund "crooks and communists." He simply was employing a classic American political tactic—confuse the issue by smearing the other guy.

There's probably no outrageous accusation that hasn't been flung in the sacred name of "win at all costs." All of our most revered presidents have been on the receiving end.

Andrew Jackson's wife was charged with being a bigamist. Thomas Jefferson's election, it was said, would set "the seal of death . . . on our holy religion," and "prostitutes . . . will preside in the sanctuaries now devoted to the worship of the Most High." Abraham Lincoln, considered by many historians to be our greatest president, was attacked as "a lowbred, obscene clown," a "dishonest baboon," and "another Benedict Arnold." Even George Washington, whose superb leadership, integrity, and good judgment have secured his place of honor in our history, was called a "tyrant," a "dictator," and an "imposter." One political cartoon even implied that he was an "ass." Washington had no intention of setting a precedent when he declined a third term. He simply refused to take any more of the abuse.

It may be true, as Confucius said, that he who slings mud loses ground, but the participants in American political campaigns obviously do not believe it. In every presidential election, we have what the Englishman Sir James Bryce in the 1880s called "the spectacle of half the honest men supporting for the headship of the nation a person whom the other half declare to be a knave."

American politicians have also used humor as a weapon. At a 1963 press conference John F. Kennedy was told by a reporter that the Republican National Committee had "adopted a resolution saying you were pretty much of a failure." Asked the reporter, "How do you feel about that?" Kennedy's reply completely destroyed the effectiveness of the resolution. "I assume it passed unanimously," he said.

Even William Jennings Bryan, the evangelical, deadly serious Democratic candidate of 1896, 1900, and 1908, got into the act. On one occasion, when asked to address a crowd of farmers from the only available elevated stage, a manure spreader, he joked, "This is the first time I have ever spoken from a Republican platform."

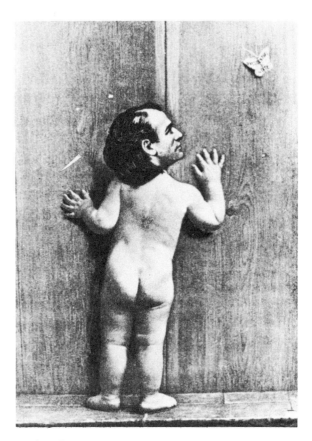

Little Billy Bryan Chasing Butterflies—an 1896 attack
on the youthful Bryan that first appeared in *Judge*.

Presidential candidates, however, must use wit carefully,
for there is a thin line between being quick on one's feet and
being a buffoon. In the 1952 campaign, Democrat Adlai
Stevenson's quips were turned against him by what he called
"the Republican law of gravity." Lincoln, whose humor is
now part of our national heritage, was roundly condemned
for telling funny stories against the tragic backdrop of the
Civil War.

While campaign rhetoric has not advanced much since the
earliest presidential elections, campaign strategies and

Lincoln as a monkey (Courtesy The Lilly Library,
Indiana University, Bloomington).

methods have changed radically throughout the years. One
welcome change is that the vice-president, although he still
presides over the Senate, no longer feels the need to take
loaded pistols to work with him as Martin Van Buren did. No
president since John Tyler has issued guns to the White
House staff to defend him against his enemies, although the

thought must have occurred to Nixon in 1973 and 1974. Indeed, we have come a long way from the relatively uncomplicated times when President Washington could say of his ambassador to France: "We haven't heard from Benjamin Franklin in Paris this year. We should write him a letter."

From Washington's day until Lincoln's day no presidential candidate campaigned openly for himself. Campaigning was considered too undignified for the aspirant to such a noble office. Lincoln even refused to vote for himself, but ·finally he was persuaded to clip his own name off the ballot and vote for the rest of his party's ticket.

Stephen A. Douglas, Lincoln's Democratic opponent in 1860, was the first candidate to stump openly, and his campaigning was offensive to most of the voters. The *Jonesboro* [Illinois] *Gazette* said at the time, "Douglas is going about peddling his opinions as a tin man peddles his ware. The only excuse for him is that as he is a small man, he has a right to be engaged in small business; and small business it is for a candidate for the Presidency to be strolling around the country begging for votes like a town constable."

Douglas, of course, was aware of the precedent he was setting and tried to maintain the fiction that his trips were nonpolitical (a practice that continues today). One of these trips was a visit he paid to his mother in Clifton Springs, New York. On this occasion a New Hampshire paper gibed that to get from Illinois to New York, he "naturally came to New Haven, Guilford, and Hartford on his way, and . . . was 'betrayed' into a speech." Again "at Worcester some Judas 'betrayed' him into a speech. At Boston, 'betrayed' again."

In some cases the candidates may have remained silent, on the theory that "it is better to keep one's mouth shut and be thought a fool than to open it and remove all doubt." For example in 1868 it was said of General Grant that he "refused to express his views, concealing the fact that he had none." No less a figure than John Adams was also guilty of such

President Grant as a drunkard and a liar.

uncharitable thoughts when he observed that "Washington got the reputation of being a great man because he kept his mouth shut." Of course, Calvin Coolidge was so noted for never saying *anything* that when the humorist Dorothy Parker was told that he had died, she quipped, "How can they tell?"

The Whig party, which was one of the two major parties from about 1832 until about 1856, specialized in keeping their candidates quiet during the campaign, leaving the hell raising to be done by others. Whig candidates (except for Henry Clay) were carefully selected generals whose views were unknown or nonexistent. An opponent remarked that "availability was the only ability" required of the Whig candidates. The strategy for a typical Whig candidate, General William Henry Harrison, in 1836 was: "Let no committee, no convention, no town meeting extract from him a single word about what he thinks now or what he will do hereafter."

An 1848 cartoon of Zachary Taylor as the Whig candidate
(typically with no qualifications)
and a general who killed many soldiers.

AN AVAILABLE CANDIDATE.
THE ONE QUALIFICATION FOR A WHIG PRESIDENT.

In the modern presidential campaign, candidates travel thousands of miles and deliver hundreds of speeches. Jet planes and television have made a great difference, but the flowery prose, the pratfalls, the outrageous gibes, and the bilge go on and on as always, and every four years we are treated to an entertaining, exciting, and wonderful show.

In spite of its "warts and all," to use one of Nixon's Watergate expressions, the presidential campaign is a uniquely American institution that has served us well. When a firm hand was essential to guide the new nation, Washington was available. Jefferson boldly doubled our country's size with the Louisiana Purchase, in spite of criticism from his short-sighted opponents who claimed, "The United States are now doomed to pay a large sum for a vast wilderness world which will . . . prove worse than useless to us." When most of the conventional wisdom (including that of young Congressman Abraham Lincoln) opposed the annexation of Texas and one major party candidate campaigned against it, James K. Polk appeared as the first dark horse candidate and won with the determination to annex not only Texas but California and the Pacific Northwest as well. At the country's most dangerous period since the dark days of Valley Forge, Lincoln emerged to conduct the struggle of the Civil War. For World War I there was Woodrow Wilson, and Franklin D. Roosevelt was in office to attack the Great Depression and to command the mightiest military force probably in the history of the world in World War II.

But no matter who has been elected to the White House, getting there has been half the fun. So let's take a long, fond glance backward at a number of the most interesting and colorful of our presidential elections—starting with the first popular contest in 1828 and finishing with a modern television extravaganza.

Look askance, if you want to, at the rhetoric, invective, and humor slung by one side at the other. But remember

WHO IS NEXT?

An 1892 lampooning of the possible Republican candidates to face Cleveland (looking on from the window). The current sitter on the pot is the incumbent president, Benjamin Harrison.

that all's fair in love and politics; and a little slander or a few well-placed potshots are as American as apple pie. What's more, there's a lot to be said in defense of a spirited and hard-fought campaign. The whole performance is, after all, designed to select the best one for the job. Even if we may not be able to agree on every qualification, certainly all our presidents have passed the muster of the Republican Chester Congdon, who said in 1916, "Damn it gentlemen, what I want for this job is a man the dogs won't urinate on."

★ ★ 2 ★ ★

OLD HICKORY

The election of 1828 was the first in which electors were popularly chosen. In the words of the candidates' detractors, it was a race between a "pimp" and a "convicted adulterer." The candidates' real names were John Quincy Adams and Andrew Jackson, and the election was almost a replay of the 1824 contest in which Adams was elected over Jackson even though Old Hickory had more electoral votes. Indeed many said the 1828 campaign lasted four years, beginning immediately after Adams was inaugurated and had appointed his cabinet.

The House of Representatives decided the 1824 election because no candidate had an electoral vote majority. The Speaker of the House, Henry Clay, had finished fourth in the election and was influential in electing Adams. General Jackson had mercilessly beaten and even killed men for lesser offenses, but he was remarkably calm this time, taking his defeat with gentlemanly good grace—at first.

Adams had all the qualifications for the presidency, unless

BORN TO COMMAND.

OF VETO MEMORY.

HAD I BEEN CONSULTED.

KING ANDREW THE FIRST.

King Andrew the First—Jackson trampling on the constitution.

political astuteness is one of them. He demonstrated this flaw in his makeup immediately by determining, upon taking office, that the man best qualified to be Secretary of State was Henry Clay. After all, Clay had been sufficiently qualified to prefer Adams over Jackson. The Jacksonians howled their indignation. They set up a cry of "corrupt bargain" that was to make Adams, like his father, a one-term president and to dog Henry Clay throughout his lifelong struggle to be president. The legislature of Tennessee, Jackson's home state, passed a resolution of condemnation: "Mr. Adams desired the office of President; he went into the combination without it, and came out with it. Mr. Clay desired that of Secretary of State; he went into the combination without it, and came out with it." Could anything be plainer? Jackson himself charged that a "bargain and sale of the constitutional rights of the people" had been effected. Of Clay's appointment Old Hickory wrote, "So you see the *Judas* of the West has closed the contract and will receive the thirty pieces of silver. His end will be the same. Was there ever witnessed such a barefaced corruption?"

The hostilities recessed briefly in 1828 for the nominations of the candidates. Since the Federalist party's death, around 1816, both major candidates had come from different wings of Jefferson's Democratic–Republican party. The Jacksonians, calling themselves Democrats, nominated John C. Calhoun as Jackson's running mate. Adams's faction nominated Richard Rush for vice-president. Rush previously had been appointed by Adams to the Treasury Department under President Monroe; a colleague had called it "the worst appointment since the Roman emperor Caligula appointed his horse Consul." There was no such objection raised this time. The battle thus was joined between:

> *John Quincy Adams, who can write,*
> *And Andrew Jackson, who can fight.*

So went a ditty of the time in a pretty valid assessment of the two candidates. Jackson was not a man of letters, as Adams observed when he referred to him as a "barbarian and savage who can scarcely spell his own name." The general believed that the earth was flat, spelled Europe "Urop," and was said to have read only one book all the way through in his life— *The Vicar of Wakefield*, oddly enough. Adams, on the other hand, was an intellectual and a very able man, but—like his father before him—he seemed to have unconcealed contempt for the voters, a flaw that is usually fatal in elected officials. For example, he once told the Congress not to give the rest of the world the impression "that we are palsied by the will of our constituents." Until he read that speech, Jackson said, he thought Adams had "a tolerable share of common sense."

The campaign was exceedingly dirty, with both sides reaching new depths of scurrility. The voters were constantly reminded of Adams's "corrupt bargain" and his "infamous Coalition" with Clay. Adams was a "usurper" of the presidency, whose chess set and billiard table, purchased with his own money, became "gaming tables and gambling furniture." Jackson was denounced as a liar, a thief, a drunkard, a bigamist, an adulterer, a gambler, a cockfighter, a Negro trader, and a murderer. The Dutch voters in Pennsylvania and New York were told by the Jacksonians, in words so solemn as to seem like documented facts, that the friends of Adams's Coalition "have heretofore spoken of the Dutch, calling them *'the black Dutch,' 'the stupid Dutch,' 'the ignorant Dutch,'* and other names equally decorous and civil."

Jackson as a hog being barbecued
on the furnace of "public opinion."

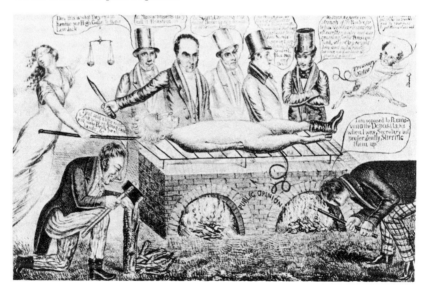

The general, on the other hand, "revered" the Dutch for their patriotism and countless other virtues. Jackson, in the eyes of the opposition, was an ignorant, cruel, bloodthirsty man, who was "quite insane." A political handbook said: "You know that he is no jurist, no statesman, no politician; that he is destitute of historical, political, or statistical knowledge; that he is unacquainted with the orthography, concord, and government of his language; you know that he is a man of no labor, no patience, no investigation; in short that his whole recommendation is animal fierceness and organic energy. He is wholly unqualified by education, habit and temper for the station of President."

In a less serious vein a Democratic newspaper published puns and jokes about the opposition.

"Hurrah for Jackson," said one man.
"Hurrah for the Devil," replied a Jackson hater.
"Very well," retorted the first man. "You stick to your candidate, and I'll stick to mine."

Many stories were told to illustrate Adams's disdain for commoners. One likened the Adams supporters among the plain people to the Frenchman who bragged that King Louis had spoken to him.

"What did the King say to you?" asked an impressed friend.
"He told me to get out of his way," was the reply.

Clay's name provided grist for the punsters. The puns were awful, of course—and in this respect little has changed since 1828.

"Why is Adams on ticklish ground?"
"Because he stands on slippery Clay."

Jackson as "Richard III: Methought the souls
of all that I had murder'd came to my tent."

   With these preliminaries and inanities taken care of, both
sides got down to serious business. The chief ammunition
against Jackson was the Coffin Hand Bill, a circular which
purported to give "Some account of some of the Bloody
Deeds of GENERAL JACKSON." It gave the names of six
soldiers who had been tried and executed shortly after the
battle of New Orleans for crimes of robbery, arson, mutiny,
and desertion. Their trials were perfectly legal, and they had
been executed strictly according to law. But the handbill
referred to them as "victims" of Old Hickory's callous

cruelty. Under each name was the picture of a huge, black coffin, and a description was given of the "murders" of the "innocent" men. Included was a poem entitled "Mournful Tragedy," which contained verses like:

Sure he will spare! Sure JACKSON yet
Will all reprieve but one—
O hark! those shrieks! that cry of death!
The deadly deed is done!

One Democrat lightheartedly challenged the Coffin Hand Bill: "Pshaw! Why don't you tell the whole truth? On the 8th

The Coffin Handbill, picturing Jackson as a murderer.

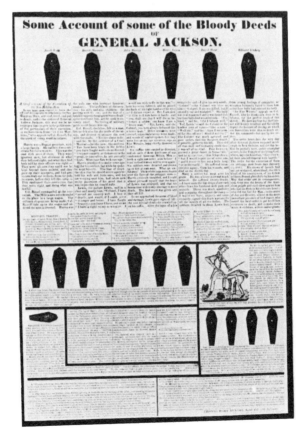

of January, 1815, he murdered in the coldest blood 1,500 British soldiers for merely trying to get into New Orleans in search of booty and beauty." Another Jackson supporter was more outraged. The public could now discern, he said, the thorough corruption of the administration. Adams and Clay conceived this "despicable broadside to strip the honored laurel from [Jackson's] brow."

Prostitution and debauchery also played a central role in the campaign. The Jacksonians circulated the story that Adams introduced a young American chambermaid to Czar Alexander when Adams was ambassador to Russia. The story was perfectly true, according to Adams, and the girl was introduced to the czar at the czar's request and in the presence of his wife. The czar was curious, said Adams, since the chambermaid had written a letter intercepted by Russian authorities recounting the czar's reputed love affairs. It was all in good humor, according to Adams, and the letter afforded the Russian royal couple "some amusement." Based on the incident, Jackson's supporters charged that Adams was "a practicing pimp," a "procurer" of American girls for the czar. The Democrats mocked Adams as "The Pimp of the Coalition," and noted that his activities as a procurer explained his fabulous success as a diplomat.

On the other side, the *Cincinnati Gazette* reported that "General Jackson's mother was a *COMMON PROSTITUTE* brought to this country by the British soldiers! She afterwards married a *MULATTO MAN*, with whom she had several children, of which General *JACKSON IS ONE!*" One issue reported that Jackson's "older brother was sold as a slave in Carolina."

The slander that most enraged Jackson was the attack on his wife, Rachel Donelson. Andrew and Rachel had married under the mistaken impression that she was legally divorced from her first husband. The couple was innocent of intentional wrongdoing, and when the awful truth was discovered shortly afterward, they dissolved the marriage. They repeated their vows four months later, after the divorce was obtained.

For the 1828 campaign the *Cincinnati Gazette* dredged up this story and charged that Jackson had prevailed upon Rachel to desert her husband and "live with him in the character of a wife." Anyone else would have been jailed for "open and notorious lewdness," but not Old Hickory. His reward was a presidential nomination. "Ought a convicted adulteress and her paramour husband to be placed in the highest offices of this free and Christian land?" asked the *Gazette.* "If General Jackson should be elected President," declared another Adams supporter, "what effect, think you, fellow-citizens, will it have upon the American youth?"

All of these charges were calculated to provoke Jackson into such a fit of rage that he would kill someone (presumably not Adams). "How hard it is to keep the cowhide from the villains," the general fumed, and he threatened to challenge Clay to a duel. Fortunately for Jackson—and doubtless for Clay—he was talked out of this notion and managed more or less to contain himself.

"Clay is managing Adams' campaign," said a Jacksonian, "not like a statesman of the cabinet, but like a shyster, pettifogging in a bastard suit before a country squire." Jackson, however, held Adams responsible. "He is certainly the basest, meanest scoundrel that ever disgraced the image of his God. Nothing is too mean or low for him to condescend to to secretly carry his cowardly and base purposes of slander into effect. Even the aged and virtuous female is not free from his secret combinations of base slander." In one of her last letters Rachel Jackson gave her views: "The enemys of the Genl have dipt their arrows in wormwood and gall and sped them at me . . . they have Disquieted one that they had no rite to do." She added that she would rather be "a doorkeeper in the house of God than to live in that palace at Washington."

On the election day both sides put on a massive get-out-the-vote drive, which would compare favorably with those of today. In New York, where Adams's fortunes had dramatically improved with the death of his archenemy, Governor De Witt Clinton (an event referred to by Clay as a "fortuitous demise"), Jackson's ally Martin Van Buren urged on his followers. He reminded them not to "forget to bet all you can." An Ohioan complained to Clay that if Tennessee "disgorges one thousand voters upon us, we are gone." He explained that his side would have only "two or three thousand illegal ones of our own." The Jacksonians were so certain of attempts at fraud that they used poll watchers, a practice that was new then but is common now.

The result was a resounding victory for Jackson, who received 178 electoral votes to 83 for Adams. The opposition did not have even the thread of hope that they were to have four years later, when Jackson won reelection by demolishing Clay. That hope was the "one comfort left: God has promised that the days of the wicked shall be short; the wicked [Jackson] is old and feeble, and he may die before [the Electoral College can meet]. It is the duty of every good Christian to pray for our Maker to have pity on us."

Jackson's victory was marred by the death of his beloved Rachel only a few weeks after the 1828 election. He blamed his enemies for her death, and at her funeral he swore: "In the presence of this dear saint I can and do forgive all my enemies. But those vile wretches who have slandered her must look to God for mercy."

Andrew Jackson was a new kind of president. Under him the country was not "ruined past redemption," as his enemies feared—but its course was thoroughly altered. He was the first popularly elected president (before him the electors were chosen largely by the legislatures and an aristocratic minority), and he acted for all the people. He left office in 1837 with, he said, but two regrets. He was sorry he didn't "shoot Henry Clay and hang John C. Calhoun." As

"Jackson is to be President, and you will be HANGED."

Jackson performing a hanging.

one historian has said of Jackson, "More than one such president a century would be hard to take. Yet he was a giant in his influence on our system . . . and second only to Washington in terms of influence on the Presidency." In a national crisis Americans might say, as men of goodwill did in 1861, "O for one hour of Andrew Jackson!"

☆ ☆ ☆ 3 ☆ ☆ ☆

TIPPECANOE AND TYLER TOO

The first truly modern campaign was probably that of 1840, called by one historian the "jolliest and most idiotic in our history." An incumbent president was attacked for taking baths, his opponent was chosen because he had no views—and a committee was formed to see that he didn't develop any—and there was a vice-presidential candidate whose main qualification seemed to be that he had once killed a man. The losing party was "sung down, lied down, and drunk down." One newspaper hoped after the election that the "buffoonery of 1840" would never again be repeated but would "stand solitary and alone, on the page of history, a damning stain on the brow of Federalism."

The incumbent president running for reelection was the Democrat Martin Van Buren, who had been handpicked by Andrew Jackson to be his successor four years earlier. Van Buren was from Kinderhook, New York, and called himself Old Kinderhook, the initials of which gave birth to the slang expression O.K. The *New York Morning Herald* unkindly

"A Hard Row to Hoe!"—Jackson leading Van Buren
back to the White House, which was "O.K."

suggested that the letters stood for Jackson's "illiterate method" of saying "Ole Kurrek (all correct)." The Democrats used
O.K. affectionately, but the Whigs turned it around to indicate what they intended to make Van Buren in November:
"K.O. for Kicked Out."

The times were wild, and invective flowed freely. William
Seward, later to be Lincoln's Secretary of State, castigated
Van Buren as "a crawling reptile, whose only claim was that
he had inveigled the confidence of a credulous, blind,
dotard, old man [Jackson]." Another critic said, "The search-
ing look of his keen eyes showed that he believed . . . that
language was given to conceal thought." History has judged
Van Buren to have been an able president who became
vulnerable to political attacks because of the hard times
caused by the Panic of 1837. It's unfortunate that he is remembered mainly for being the first president born under
our constitution, for coining a new slang expression, and for
bathing regularly.

The Whigs nominated General William Henry Harrison,

A hostile view of Van Buren.

whose principal virtues were that he had no known views and was a military hero. (A "hero of forty defeats," his enemies said.) He was also the titular head of the party, having lost to Van Buren in the previous election of 1836. By 1840 he was sixty-eight years old—the oldest candidate ever nominated for the presidency by a major party until Ronald Reagan in 1980.

Harrison was the commanding general at the battle of Tippecanoe in 1811. He defeated the Indian chief Tecumseh, who was defending the Indians' hunting grounds against encroachment by the white man. Harrison became known as Old Tippecanoe and was presidential timber from that point on. (In those days all the generals were called old something or other, like today's bourbon whiskeys. Andrew Jackson was known as Old Hickory; Zachary Taylor, Old Rough and Ready; and Winfield Scott, Old Fuss and Feathers.)

The Whigs chose John Tyler, a Democrat, as Harrison's

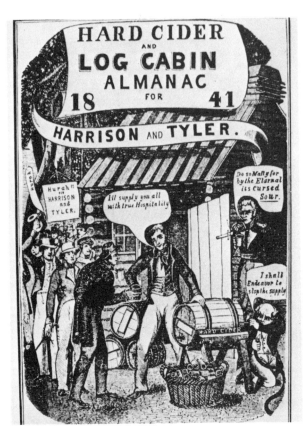

"Hurrah for Old Tippecanoe."

running mate. The battle cry of 1840 thus became "Tippecanoe and Tyler too." A Whig who cared little for Tyler said of the addition to the ticket, "There was rhyme but no reason in it."

Henry Clay, who coveted the Whig nomination and had fully expected to get it, was furious at the selection of Harrison. "My friends are not worth the powder and shot it would take to kill them!" he exclaimed. "If there were two Henry Clays, one of them would make the other President of the United States. . . . I am the most unfortunate man in the history of parties: always run by my friends when sure to be defeated, and now betrayed for a nomination when I, or any one, would be sure of an election." The *New Orleans Bee* agreed: "Just think of a man such as Mr. Clay . . . without whom the Whig party would not this day exist, cast aside for a driveller."

As for the Democrats, their incumbent vice-president, Richard M. Johnson, was said actually to have killed Tecumseh. It also was said that he "openly and shamefully lives in adultery with a buxom young Negro." This and other rumors lost him the support of Jackson, who predicted, "If Col Johnson is the nominee it will loose [*sic*] the democracy [i.e., the Democratic party] thousand [*sic*] of votes." The convention therefore decided not to renominate Johnson—indeed it nominated no one for the vice-presidency—but he was allowed to run on his own. This he did, with the slogan, "Rumpsey-dumpsey, rumpsey-dumpsey. Colonel Johnson killed Tecumseh."

This rhythmic couplet, a holdover from the 1836 election, was a portent of things to come. The *Baltimore Republican* set the tone of the campaign when it published the reaction of a disgruntled Clay disciple to Harrison's nomination: "Get rid of . . . [Harrison]! and pray tell . . . how are we to do it?" The writer of the article supplied the answer, "Give him a barrel of hard cider, and settle a pension of two thousand a year on him, and my word for it, he will sit the remainder of his days in a log cabin by the side of a 'seacoal' fire and study moral philosophy."

The Democrats republished this piece of foolishness to taunt the Whigs, but the latter seized on it as an opportunity sent from heaven. They made Harrison the "log cabin and hard cider candidate" and also made the Democrats look like the party of the rich. "General Harrison is sneered at by the Eastern office-holders' pimps, as the 'Log-Cabin Candidate,' " declared one Whig newspaper. "Never mind! [Log-cabin dwellers] have a way of taking care of themselves, when insulted, which has sometimes surprised folks." Ano-

Jackson and Van Buren as "Uncle Sam's Pet Pups,"
being trapped by General Harrison.

ther said, "Log-Cabin Candidate is the term of reproach . . .
[of] pampered office-holders . . . [who] sneer at the idea of
making a *poor man* President of the United States." Actually, Harrison was far from poor—he lived in a mansion on
the Ohio River—but this made no difference to anybody.

After that the Whigs did not need to debate the issues or to
try to hide the fact that their candidate had no views. They
simply used the slogans of log cabins and hard cider and
made up countless songs to drown out anyone who tried to
talk sense. As the Whig managers correctly observed, "Pas-
sion and prejudice, properly aroused and directed, will do
about as well as principle and reason in a party contest."
Modern campaign techniques, as some cynics would say,
thus were first used in the election of 1840.

What about the issue of the independent treasury? The
Whigs replied:

Hush-a-bye-baby;
Daddy's a Whig.
Before he comes home
Hard cider he'll swig.

Was Harrison planning to reestablish the national bank?

Let Van from his coolers of silver drink wine
And lounge on his cushioned settee,
Our man on a buckeye bench can recline,
Content with hard cider is he.

There were enough Whig rhymes and songs to fill a book. Horace Greeley collected the most popular ones and published them in the *Log Cabin Song Book*, which became the psalmbook of the campaign.

The Whigs held mass meetings, measuring attendance by the acre: "Six acres of men heard General Harrison." They organized parades with floats exhibiting log cabins and barrels of hard cider. Campaign souvenirs and merchandise, featuring such items as Tippecanoe Shaving Soap, Log Cabin Emollient, Harrison and Tyler neckties, and pocket brandy and whiskey bottles in the shape of log cabins, were sold everywhere. The Old Cabin Whiskey in these unique containers was supplied by the E.C. Booz Distillery, which contributed to the language another word, booze, for liquor.

With all their electioneering gimmicks, the Whigs still had time for Van Buren. He was called Sweet Sandy Whiskers and was ridiculed as a fop "laced up in corsets, such as women in town wear, and, if possible, tighter than the best of them." The most vicious attacks were launched by Davy Crockett and Congressman Charles Ogle, with the latter delivering a three-day speech in the House on "The Regal Splendor of the President's Palace." According to Ogle, the

White House "palace" grounds had rare plants and shrubs, and "clever sized hills" constructed in pairs "to resemble . . . an Amazon's bosom, with a miniature knoll or hillock on its apex, to denote the nipple." The inside of the White House contained "silk tassels, galloon, gimp and satin medallion to beautify and adorn the Blue Elliptical Saloon." The climax came when Ogle revealed that a bathtub had been installed in the White House and that Van Buren was "the first President [to insist upon] the pleasures of the warm or tepid bath [as] proper accompaniments of a palace life."

Ogle's speech was made up of lies, of course (except, one would hope, the part about Van Buren's taking baths), but this did not deter the Whigs from using it and taunting the Democrats with it throughout the campaign. The speech was serialized on the front pages of leading newspapers, and Whig speakers traveled with it in their saddlebags. "Mr. Van Buren was in such a rage at reading Mr. Ogle's speech," a Louisville paper said, "that he actually burst his corset."

To counter the Democratic charges that he was "an imbecile on leading strings," Harrison decided to make speeches himself, thereby becoming the first presidential candidate to stump. It was hardly out-and-out stumping as Douglas did it in 1860, or as we know it today. He "was not actually let loose," one Democrat asserted, "but the rope only a little lengthened, like that of a pet 'possum, to exercise his limbs."

He spoke chiefly on safe issues like monarchy in government, which he was foursquare against, and he urged citizens to effect reform "peacefully if you can," for otherwise "the tyrants of Europe" would rejoice. Occasionally his practice of speaking out of both sides of his mouth got him into trouble—or would have in a sane campaign. He wrote a northern congressman, for instance, that the suggestion that he favored slavery was a vile slander, and to a southerner he said that he had "done and suffered more to support Southern rights than any person north of Mason and Dixon's line."

He urged each correspondent to keep the opinions he expressed confidential. At length a committee was formed to screen Harrison's correspondence and make sure that a "cuckoo did not fly out of his mouth."

An army of Whigs took to the hustings to praise Old Tippecanoe. One defender was a former representative, Seargent S. Prentiss of Mississippi, who was proud to defend such causes as "the fair flower of womanhood" from the "pestilential effluvia" of the Democrats. On one occasion a Van Buren supporter hissed as Prentiss was delivering his usual vitriol. Prentiss stopped, pointed at his detractor, and announced, "Rome was once saved by the hissing of a goose, but I doubt if this republic ever will be."

Harrison and Tyler won the election by a big electoral vote margin. An incredible seventy-eight percent of the eligible voters went to the polls, no doubt because of the lively campaign. But the defeated side claimed that the "vast increase in votes" was accomplished by "mercenaries— hired, bribed and purchased wretches which the corruption fund has secured for the Whig ticket."

After the weird campaign was over, and it was "O.K." for Van Buren to return to Kinderhook, one newspaper editor expressed the hope that "No more may the world see coons, cabins, and cider usurp the place of principles, nor doggerel verse elicit a shout, while argument, principle and reason are passed by with a derisive sneer." After every campaign there are always such hopes.

As an epilogue to the "jolly" and "idiotic" election of 1840, Harrison was inaugurated on March 4, 1841 and died a month later—"the deed of a kind and overruling Providence," according to Jackson. The official cause of death was pneumonia, but some cynics said Harrison died of doctors. The medical men "blistered" and "cupped" him, and administered opium, camphor, brandy, crude petroleum, and snake weed. Since the last two were Indian medicine men's remedies, Harrision may have been finished, as one historian said, by "Tecumseh's revenge." The redoubtable poet William Cullen Bryant, in one of his lesser-known efforts, regretted Harrison's death "only because he did not live long enough to prove his incapacity for the office of President."

★ ★ ★ 4 ★ ★ ★

FIFTY-FOUR FORTY OR FIGHT

The Whigs were denied the fruits of their tumultuous 1840 campaign victory by the early death of President Harrison. Not only were both houses of Congress Democratic but thanks to the Whigs' determination to straddle the issues, the Democrat John Tyler, whom they chose as Harrison's running mate, was now president. President Tyler, or "His Accidency," as his enemies called him, proceeded to act more like a Jacksonian Democrat than a Whig, with the result that at the end of his term he was, in the words of the New York boss Thurlow Weed, "the poor, miserable, despised imbecile, who now goes from the Presidential chair, scorned of all parties."

The Whigs were determined to run more conventional candidates in the 1844 campaign. They nominated sixty-seven-year-old Henry Clay, who had lusted after the presidency all his adult life, giving him his third and apparently, his last nomination. One of Clay's claims to fame was his statement, "I would rather be right than President," which one writer labeled "the sourest grape since Aesop originated his fable."

For vice-president the Whigs nominated Theodore Frelinghuysen, "a Christian gentleman," who was selected to balance Clay's "fluent profanity" and "known fondness for drinking and gambling."

The Democrats nominated James K. Polk—the first dark horse candidate—for president and George M. Dallas for vice-president. The party thus passed over "a man of ability like Van Buren" and in the words of the *National Intelligencer*, "let itself down" to Polk. "A more ridiculous, contemptible and forlorn candidate was never put forth by any party," said the *New York Herald*.

"Who the hell is Polk?" the Whigs gleefully shouted, making this their campaign cry. Clay had another view, though he kept it private. He had known Polk in Congress,

Clay and Polk as "Political Cockfighters."

and on the occasion of Polk's retirement as Speaker of the House in 1839, Clay had jeered from the galleries, "Go home, God damn you! Go home where you belong!" The story is told that Clay was relaxing at his home when his son rushed in and asked him to guess who had received the Democratic nomination. "Why, Matty [Van Buren], of course," said Clay. "No, guess again." "Cass?" "No." "Buchanan?" "No." Then Clay laughed, "Don't tell me they've been such fools as to take Calhoun or Johnson." His son again said no, and the exasperated Clay demanded, "Then who the devil is it?" When he heard the name "James K. Polk," he slowly poured himself a drink, sat down, and said, "Beat again, by God!"

The main issue of the campaign was the annexation of Texas, or to use the phrase of the times, the "reannexation" of Texas. Both Van Buren and Clay, the leaders of their respective parties, were against annexation, and in Van Buren's case it lost him his party's nomination. Before the convention Clay wrote that he considered annexation "as a measure compromising the national character, involving us certainly in a war with Mexico." As the campaign progressed, however, he saw that his stand was unpopular, and by the end of July he stated, "I have no hesitation in saying that, far from having any personal objection to the annexation of Texas, I should be glad to see it, without dishonor, without war."

His attitude angered the northern Whig leaders who wanted the issue to be "Polk, slavery, and Texas," versus "Clay, Union, and liberty." One Whig declared that Clay "is rotten as a stagnant fish pond... and always has been. Confound him and all his compromises from first to last." Two days later, Clay, unnerved by the reaction, declared flatly that "I am decidedly opposed to the immediate annexation of Texas to the United States." He added that his statements "were not inconsistent," and that he would "write no further letters for publication on any public question." His flip-flops provided the Democratic press with a field day. Stealing the idea of verse from the Whigs of 1840, one editor wrote of Clay:

> *He wires in and wires out,*
> *And leaves the people still in doubt,*
> *Whether the snake that made the track,*
> *Was going South, or coming back.*

The Democrats shrewdly advocated not only the "reannexation of Texas" but also the "reoccupation of Oregon." The *re* was used to establish the claims that Oregon was ours by settlement and treaty and that Texas was originally part of the Louisiana Purchase. In the case of Oregon, Polk campaigned for the entire territory up to latitude 54°40′ north, giving rise to the Democratic campaign slogan, "Fifty-Four Forty or Fight." (As president, he later settled for the forty-ninth parallel, but he got all of Mexico north of the Rio Grande River.)

The campaign was not nearly as lively as that of 1840, since the Whigs seemed to have lost some of their ardor. There was, however, enough vitriol to go around. Clay was called morally unfit for the presidency and said to be a duelist, a heavy drinker, and an inordinate gambler, who was the inventor of the poker game. Polk was "an infidel from Tennessee" (the last part of which was true), a slaveholder who abused his slaves, a haughty tyrant, a pliant tool, and a petty scoundrel. "Clay spends his days at a gaming table and his nights in a brothel," one Democrat said. Another said Clay's standard should be "a pistol, a pack of cards, and a brandy bottle." The *New York American* said that someone had seen "Polk's slaves on their way to die in the sugar mills of Louisiana" with "JKP burned into their flesh." Another paper said that the annexation of Texas, favored by Polk, was "a step

Tyler as an ass, Polk as a goose, and Van Buren as a fox,
auctioned off by Clay "for want of use."

conceived by traitors and base conspirators against the
Union."

Clay was castigated by one Democrat as "notorious for his
fiendish and vindictive speech, for his disregard of the most
important moral obligations, for his blasphemy, for his
gambling propensities, and for his frequent and bloodthirsty attempts upon the lives of his fellow-men." This
Democratic propagandist went on to say that Clay had violated all of the Ten Commandments and gave examples—
except for those, such as "Mr. Clay's debaucheries and
midnight revelries in Washington," that were "too shocking,
too disgusting to appear in public print."

The voters, it seemed, had little choice as far as religious
morality was concerned, what with Clay's repeated "viola-
tions of the decalogue" on the one hand, and the "infidel"
Polk on the other. It was pointed out that Polk came by his
impiety honestly, as anyone could see from the epitaph of his
grandfather Ezekiel Polk, which was clearly carved on "dur-

able wood" and was standing above his grave. It was a twenty-line poem that Ezekiel had composed himself, containing such couplets as:

> *To holy cheats was never willing*
> *To give one solitary shilling;*
>
> *First Fruits and tenths are odious things,*
> *So are bishops, priests and kings.*

Polk up a tree, calculated to hearten Whigs and discourage Democrats.

On the lighter side, the Democrats used slogans and songs, as the Whigs had four years earlier. The Whigs were referred to as "coons," a favorite term of Andrew Jackson. The Democrats called themselves "coon skinners of 1844." In answer to the Whig question "Who is Polk?" they replied, "The K in Col. Polk's name is understood to stand for 'Koon-killer.'" They set this rhyme to music and sang it in the streets:

> *Blow the trumpet, beat the drum*
> *Run Clay coons, we come. We come.*

Polk won the election by the narrow margin of 1,337,243 votes against Clay's 1,299,062. When New York's 36 electoral votes were still in doubt, Polk had 134 electoral votes to Clay's 105. Eventually Polk won New York, and the election, by 4,000 votes. Young Abraham Lincoln, at the time an ardent Whig, lamented that if an abolitionist third party had not been in the field, New York would have "voted with us . . . Mr. Clay would now be President . . . and Texas not annexed." True enough, but if the ticket of Polk and Dallas had not prevailed, the second-largest city in Texas today might carry the name of Santa Anna, or even worse, Frelinghuysen.

Another future president who did not share Polk's enthusiasm for Texas, Oregon, and California was General Zachary Taylor, who succeeded Polk. Taylor and Polk made a "strangely contrasting pair" in March, 1849, as they rode together down Pennsylvania Avenue for Taylor's inauguration: Polk, the studious, "proud master of every detail of the Presidency," and Taylor, the rough, unsophisticated old soldier. The outgoing president must have winced at Taylor's casual remark that "California and Oregon are both too far away." The "people out there" should be allowed to "form

"This is the House that Polk Built"—
indicating how frail Polk's support was for his schemes.

an independent government of their own." At the end of the
ceremony, Polk said to the new president, "I hope, sir, the
country will be prosperous under your administration," but
in his diary he wrote that Taylor "was exceedingly ignorant of
public affairs, and . . . of very ordinary capacity."

Who was James K. Polk? He was the president who ful-
filled America's Manifest Destiny by expanding its borders
across the continent from the Atlantic to the Pacific. "No
man and no administration was ever more assailed, and none

ever achieved more," said the *New York Sun* upon Polk's death. It is ironic that for all his accomplishments, Polk was vilified at the end of his term as "Polk the Mendacious" and "the little mole." Three months later he died of "chronic diarrhea."

Andrew Jackson's comment could be Polk's epitaph. The old general was overjoyed when Polk was elected and sent him the following message: "Who is j.k. polk will be no more asked by the coons—A.J." Who indeed was James K. Polk? He was the only strong president between Jackson and Lincoln. He knew what he wanted to do; it was more than almost any other president has ever done; he said he could do it in only one term; and he did it.

★ ★ 5 ★ ★

HONEST ABE

"Mr. Lincoln is already beaten," said Horace Greeley in August, 1864. "He cannot be elected. And we must have another ticket to save us from utter overthrow." The *New York World* said, "Honest old Abe has few honest men to defend his honesty." These were two of the more charitable views of Abraham Lincoln and his chances for reelection in the summer of 1864. The Army of the Potomac was bogged down in a war of attrition before Richmond, Sherman was still a good distance from Atlanta, and to the average voter the end of the hated Civil War was nowhere in sight. Potatoes were $160 per bushel, cabbages were $10 per head, and gold was selling for over $270 an ounce. As Calvin Coolidge was to say in 1931 during the Great Depression, "the country was not in good shape."

Lincoln himself despaired of winning the coming election. "It seems exceedingly probable," he wrote in a sealed document for his cabinet, "that this Administration will not be re-elected. Then it will be my duty to cooperate with the President-elect, as to save the Union between the election and the inauguration, as he will have secured his election on such ground that he cannot possibly save it afterward."

Even Lincoln's political friends thought he was a misfit in the presidency. Said one Republican senator, "We went in for a rail-splitter, and we have got one." Another party leader declared that most Republicans were Lincoln men "from pure necessity" and were eager to "get a competent, loyal President, in the place of our present imbecile incumbent." Even a cabinet member—Secretary of War Stanton—publicly referred to the president as "a low, cunning clown," and Lockwood Todd, a nephew of Mrs. Lincoln, thought it "disgraceful" that Lincoln was in the family. He added that he "would not vote for him to save him from hell." Greeley reminded a Massachusetts senator of the theological book containing "Chapter One—Hell; Chapter Two—Hell Continued," and added, "That gives a hint of the way Old Abe ought to be talked to in this crisis."

To the Democrats, Lincoln was a spineless, imbecilic, "awful woeful ass," a "dictator," a "coarse, vulgar joker," a "grotesque baboon," and "a third-rate lawyer who once split rails and now splits the Union." Indeed to hear the opposition tell it, the South seceded because of Lincoln's election, and if he were reelected, the South would fight on "for another thirty years."

The more extreme Peace Democrats were willing to allow slavery to continue if necessary to end the war, and they had many followers in the North. A speaker in Mount Vernon, Ohio, castigated Lincoln for continuing the war and "thus, even in the agony . . . of our national demise," flinging "away the hopes and interests of this nation." "God damn him" was heard in the crowd, amid laughter and cheers. And in the same town a farmer's wife would say repeatedly to her children, "Lincoln! how I loathe that name between my lips!"

The first nominating convention of 1864 was a rump convention of radical Republicans who thought that Lincoln was soft on the South. Its managers predicted a "giant mass rally," but only 158 faithful signed the register. The *Detroit Tribune* jeered, "Were the immortal 158 the masses? Truly answers Echo—Them Asses!" Be that as it may, the convention nominated as its presidential candidate John C. Fremont, a Union general and the Republican party's standard-bearer in its first election try in 1856.

The regular Lincoln Republicans and the War Democrats formed an alliance, which they called the National Union Party. The *New York Herald* called them "a gathering of ghouls, vultures, hyenas and other feeders upon carrion [authorized by] the great ghoul at Washington." Their logic in supporting Lincoln, the *Herald* went on, was that he "had killed so many men he ought to be allowed another term to kill as many more."

The National Unionists held their convention in June. They nominated Lincoln and as his running mate, Andrew Johnson of Tennessee, a War Democrat. Johnson appealed to Lincoln as one who would add balance to the ticket, but Thaddeus Stevens, the radical Republican Congressman, was incensed at the choice. "Can't you get a candidate for Vice President," he asked, "without going down into a damned rebel province for one?" Other Republicans thought Johnson was a "clownish drunk" and "dirty as cart-wheel grease," but Lincoln wanted him, and he was the choice of the convention.

Democratic newspapers didn't care for either member of the ticket, calling them such names as "a rail-splitting buffoon and a boorish tailor, both from the backwoods, both growing up in uncouth ignorance." The *New York World* called the nomination of these "two ignorant, boorish, third-rate backwoods lawyers" an "insult to the common sense of the people," and added, "The age of statesmen is gone...."

God save the Republic . . . from the buffoon and gawk . . . we
have for President." The *Chicago Times* reprinted the *Richmond Dispatch* editorial comment, "We say of Old Abe it
would be impossible to find such another ass in the United
States, and therefore, we say let him stay."

Lincoln said of his renomination, "I do not allow myself to
suppose that . . . the convention [has decided] that I am
either the greatest or best man in America, but rather they
have concluded it is not best to swap horses while crossing
the river." Many people were mystified, Lincoln said, that
he would want a renomination, which "reminded him of a
story." An itinerant preacher asked an official for permission
to speak in Springfield, Lincoln's hometown, "on the second
coming of our Savior. 'Oh, bosh,' said the official, 'if our
Savior had ever been to Springfield and got away with his
life, he'd be too smart to think of coming back again.' "

The Democratic convention, or as the Republicans called
it, "the Jeff Davis convention," nominated General George
B. McClellan for president. Little Mac, as he was called by
his friends—and also by his enemies, except that they ac-
cented different words—accepted the nomination. He repudiated its peace platform, however, which called for the
armies to cease hostilities and go home: The "Southern
States would then be asked to join a convention to restore the
Union." The question of what to do if they refused was not
addressed.

Little Mac had been a thorn in Lincoln's side earlier in the
war when he was the commander of the Army of the Potomac. He had a reputation for action; but to Lincoln's dismay,
his commanding general continually prepared his troops to
fight but never seemed willing to lead them into battle.
McClellan's men did so much "digging in" that cartoonists
depicted Little Mac with a shovel rather than a sword. "To
fight is not his forte," Lincoln finally decided. Harry Truman
put it in more descriptive terms a century later: "McClellan

just sat on his ass," he said. The general's delays and excuses depressed Lincoln. To a friend's remark about the Army of the Potomac, Lincoln retorted, "So it is called, but that is a mistake; it is McClellan's bodyguard." On another particularly exasperating occasion, he wrote McClellan a note saying, "If you don't want to use the army I should like to borrow it."

Finally McClellan engaged Robert E. Lee at Antietam in one of the bloodiest battles of the war. Had McClellan been more daring, Lincoln believed, he could have smashed Lee's army and ended the war, but his caution allowed Lee to escape. Instead of pursuing and destroying the Confederate army, McClellan regrouped and complained of "sore-tongued and fatigued horses." Lincoln, in a sarcastic reply, asked, "Will you pardon me for asking what the horses of your army have done since the battle of Antietam that fatigues anything?"

McClellan was not content to assume all the military responsibilities. He also insisted on giving Lincoln advice on how to run the government. Once after receiving one of McClellan's messages, Lincoln was asked what he intended to do about McClellan's attempted interference. "Nothing," Lincoln responded, "but it made me think of the man whose horse kicked up and stuck his foot through the stirrup. He said to the horse, 'If you are going to get on I will get off.' "

Lincoln ended McClellan's army career after Antietam. "I said I would remove him if he let Lee's army get away from him," Lincoln said, "and I must do so. He has got the slows."

The campaign of 1864 was fiercely fought and extremely dirty. The Republicans, who were considered to be the underdogs at first, began the campaign by charging that all who had attended the Democratic convention were rebels or rebel sympathizers and that the convention and platform were treasonable. The considered opinion of the *New York*

Times was that every man at the convention was a "black-hearted traitor." So successful were the Republicans with the charge of treason that a contemporary historian wrote: "[the Democratic party] has the taint of disloyalty, which whether true or false will cling to it, like the poisoned shirt of Nessus, for a century." The historian's idea was right but his timing was wrong—the taint only lasted twenty years.

McClellan kicked off the Democrats' campaign with the statement: "The President is nothing more than a well-meaning baboon. He is the original gorilla. What a specimen to be at the head of our affairs!"

An anti-Lincoln biography was published anonymously, with the intention of making Lincoln look completely ridiculous. After giving a history of his early years and his political career, the biographer ended with this physical description: "When speaking [Lincoln] reminds one of the old signal-telegraph that used to stand on Staten Island. His head is shaped something like a ruta-bago, and his complexion is that of a Saratoga trunk. His hands and feet are plenty large enough, and in society he has the air of having too many of them. . . . In his habits he is by no means foppish, though he brushes his hair sometimes, and is said to wash. . . . He can hardly be called handsome, though he is certainly much better looking since he had the small-pox."

"[Lincoln] stands six feet twelve in his socks, which he changes once every ten days," ran a popular description of the time. "His anatomy is composed mostly of bones, and when walking he resembles the offspring of a happy marriage between a derrick and a windmill."

Harsh criticism of Lincoln extended even to his Gettysburg Address, acclaimed today as one of the most beautiful pieces of prose in American literature. When it was delivered in a dedication ceremony in November 1863, it was roundly condemned. The *Harrisburg Patriot and Union* in its account of the day's activities, said, "We pass over the silly remarks of the President; for the credit of the nation we are willing that the veil of oblivion shall be dropped over them and that they shall no more be repeated or thought of." The *London Times* said, "The ceremony was rendered ludicrous by some of the sallies of that poor President Lincoln." The *Chicago Times* reported, "The cheek of every American must tingle with shame as he reads the silly, flat, and dishwatery utterances of the man who has to be pointed out to intelligent foreigners as the President of the United States. Lincoln cannot speak five grammatical sentences in succession." (The *Chicago Tribune*, however, observed that "the dedicatory remarks by President Lincoln will live among the annals of men.")

Lincoln was attacked repeatedly for his humor and depicted in cartoons as being a clown at the most inappropriate times and places. One cartoon in *Harper's Weekly* showed Lincoln facing Columbia, a forerunner of Uncle Sam, who is asking, "Where are my 15,000 sons—murdered at Fredericksburg?" Lincoln is answering, "This reminds me of a little joke." Another cartoon showed Lincoln and his friend Ward Hill (Marshall) Lamon on the battlefield at Antietam, with dead and wounded men lying all around them. Lincoln is asking Lamon to "give us that song about Picayune Butler," a ribald song of the time, while McClellan interrupts his ministering to the wounded to say, "I would prefer to hear it some other place and time."

The Republican defenders were also busy. Most of them took the tack that McClellan himself was not a "traitor" like the Peace Democrats but merely a fool who was doing their bidding. "The imbecility of McClellan," one said, "will surrender [the country] to the traitors' hands." Others were bolder and lumped Little Mac in with the traitors: "It is true that their treason is more open and noisy than his, but his is nevertheless as real and earnest as theirs." A good number of the Republican attacks on McClellan were calculated to

Lincoln attacked for fabricated levity
in the midst of Civil War horror.
McClellan is administering to a wounded soldier and saying
he would rather hear the ribald song "some other place and time."

make him look ridiculous rather than malicious. One cartoon
showed Lincoln holding McClellan (equipped with his
standard shovel) in the palm of his hand and saying, "This
reminds me of a little joke." McClellan's habit of stationing
himself far behind the battle lines also provided ammunition
for his detractors. So far behind the lines was he, one opponent said, that "in the retreat General McClellan for the first
time in his life was found in the front."

Lincoln used wit as a means of bearing his burden, as on
the occasion when he was told by a temperance advocate that
General U.S. Grant, a tenacious fighter, was careless in his
dress and drank to excess. "What are you going to do about
it?" the man asked. "Find out what he drinks," Lincoln
replied, "and send a barrel of it to my other generals." On
another occasion a visitor to the White House professed

McClellan with his shovel reminding Lincoln of "a little joke."

astonishment at finding Mr. Lincoln blacking his own shoes. "Whose shoes," asked Lincoln, "did you expect to find me blacking?" Lincoln, like all presidents, was accused of being two-faced, to which he replied, "Now I ask you, if I had another face, would I be using this one?"

A number of pamphlets were published by both sides in which biblical parallels were used for ridicule. The Democrats had one entitled *The Lincoln Catechism* that put forth questions and then gave the answers. "What is the constitution? A compact with hell, now obsolete. By whom hath the Constitution been made obsolete? By Abraham Africanus the First. To what end? That his days may be long in office. . . . Was Mr. Lincoln ever distinguished as a military officer? He was, in the Black Hawk War. What high military position did

"I Knew Him, Horatio, a Fellow of Infinite Jest,"
says "Hamlet" McClellan of Lincoln.

he hold in that war? He was a cook.... Have the loyal leagues [the Republicans] a prayer? They have: Father Abraham, who art in Washington, of glorious memory since the date of the proclamation to free negroes. Thy kingdom come, and overthrow the republic; thy will be done and the laws perish. Give us this day our daily supply of greenbacks. Forgive us our plunders, but destroy the Copperheads [Southern sympathizers]. Lead us into fat pastures; but deliver us from the eye of detectives, and make us the equal of the negro; for such shall be our kingdom, and the glory of thy administration."

The Republicans replied with *The Copperhead Catechism*. "What is the chief aim of a Copperhead in this life? To abuse the President, vilify the Administration, and glorify himself. What are the articles of thy belief? I believe in One Country, One Constitution, One Destiny; and in George B.

McClellan, who was born of respectable parents; Suffered under Edwin M. Stanton; Was refused reinforcements and descended into the swamps of Chickahominy; He was driven therefrom by fire and by sword, and upon the seventh day of battle ascended Malvern Hill, from whence he withdrew to Harrison's Landing, where he rested many days; He returned to the Potomac, fought the Battle of Antietam, and entered into Oblivion; From this he shall one day arise and be elevated to the Presidential chair, there to dispense his favors unto all who follow him. I also believe in the unalienable doctrine of State Rights, And I finally believe in a Peace which is beyond everybody's understanding."

"Don't swap horses in the middle of the stream," is a neat political slogan, and it has been used by every incumbent president since Lincoln. What really got Lincoln reelected in 1864, however, was the drastic improvement in Union fortunes in the war. On September 3, when Lincoln's position looked the gloomiest, General William T. Sherman dispatched the message: "Atlanta is ours and fairly won." Shortly afterward came the news that Admiral Farragut had captured Mobile, after storming into Mobile Bay with the battle cry, "Damn the torpedoes. Full speed ahead."

"Sherman and Farragut have knocked the bottom out of the [Democratic] nominations," said Secretary of State Seward. Horace Greeley announced that henceforth his paper would "fly the banner" of Lincoln. "I shall fight like a savage in this campaign," he said, adding, "I hate McClellan." What a difference a few days made!

The Democrats continued to try, however, with slogans like: Hurrah for Lincoln! And a rope to hang him!; Time to swap horses, November 8th; No more vulgar jokes; and His election [in 1860] was a very sorry joke [itself]. The usual fun was made of his physical appearance. "But," replied the Republicans, "if all the ugly men in the United States vote for him, he will surely be elected!"

The election was held on November 8, and the result was decisive. Lincoln won with 2,213,665 votes, against 1,802,237 for McClellan. The electoral vote was a landslide: 212 to 21. McClellan carried only the states of Kentucky, New Jersey, and Delaware, prompting one partisan to say, "Behold! For Mac one full-grown pair of states, and also—Delaware."

The inauguration on March 4, 1865 was a great triumph for Lincoln. The war, for all practical purposes, was over, and Lincoln offered conciliation to the South: "With malice toward none, with charity for all, with firmness in the right as God gives us to see the right, let us strive on to finish the work we are in, to bind up the nation's wounds, to care for him who shall have borne the battle, and for his widow and his orphan, to do all which may achieve and cherish a just and lasting peace among ourselves and with all nations."

On April 7, 1865, Lincoln dispatched a message to Grant: "General Sheridan says 'If the thing is pressed I think that Lee will surrender.' Let the thing be pressed." Two days later Lee surrendered and the war was over, but Lincoln was not to have the chance to "bind up the nation's wounds." On April 14 he was shot by an assassin. He died early the next morning.

Abraham Lincoln had saved the Union. Once again the American political system had risen to the occasion and produced a great leader when less than greatness would have meant disaster. Secretary of War Stanton's words for the sorrowing nation are an eloquent and fitting epitaph: "Now he belongs to the ages."

★ ★ 6 ★ ★

THE STOLEN ELECTION

A notable year in American history was 1876. It was the year the first electric lamp burned in Washington, the year General Custer wondered "where all those damned Indians came from" at Little Bighorn, and the centennial anniversary of the nation's birth. There was one other noteworthy event of 1876: It was the year of perhaps the only stolen presidential election.

There is some controversy about whether it was the *only* election stolen. Boss Thurlow Weed was heard to say on the results of the 1856 election that "Buchanan's margin of victory was fifty-thousand dollars." The election of 1888, in which Benjamin Harrison ousted the incumbent Grover Cleveland, was also extremely close. In fact, Cleveland outpolled Harrison in the popular vote but lost the electoral vote. On the day after the election, Harrison expressed his thanks that "Providence has given us the victory." Boss Matthew Quay, a staunch party supporter, was infuriated by Harrison's innocent remark. Said Quay, "Think of the man!

He ought to know that Providence hadn't a damn thing to do with it." He added, with candor, that Harrison would never know how many men "were compelled to approach the gates of the penitentiary to make him President."

The last year of President U.S. Grant's second term was 1876, and fraud and corruption dominated the headlines. It was felt generally that Grant himself was honest but acted like a "wooden-Indian President" who saw nothing as scandal followed scandal and grafters and thieves looted the treasury and debauched the country. Moreover, whenever one of the culprits was caught, Grant was the first to defend him. There were land grabs, salary grabs, whiskey frauds, banking scandals, mine scandals, and the famous Crédit Mobilier scandal in which a holding company was set up with the stated purpose of building the Union Pacific Railroad, but with the real purpose of fleecing the government. One enterprising thief, the United States minister to Brazil, restive because he was remote from the looting at home, defrauded the Brazilian government of $100,000.

Grant plainly wanted a third term and therefore made statements to the effect that he did not want it. "Now for the third term," he said, "I do not want it any more than I did the first. . . . I would not accept a nomination if it were tendered, unless it should be under such circumstances as to make it an imperative duty." This "declination with a string to it" was accepted promptly by both parties with a House of Representatives resolution declaring that a third-term attempt "would be unwise, unpatriotic, and fraught with peril to our free institutions." Since the resolution passed by a vote of 233 to 18, Grant felt it wise to withdraw from the fray.

With Grant out of the way, the Republicans gathered in Cincinnati in June for their convention. The leading candidate was Congressman James G. Blaine of Maine, but he was tainted with the Crédit Mobilier and a host of other scandals. He had just "exonerated" himself of the Crédit Mobilier charges with what a fellow congressman called "one of the most consummate pieces of acting that ever occurred upon any stage on earth," when fresh corruption charges were made in connection with the Little Rock and Fort Smith Railroad Company.

Blaine also had the misfortune of suffering sunstroke before the convention formally got under way, and he had to be confined to his bed. His opponents naturally visited him and "had no hesitation in predicting that he would be dead within a week, or if not dead, utterly incapable of . . . bearing any strain," such as that of being president.

In spite of, or perhaps because of, these dire predictions, Blaine recovered and was put up for the nomination at the convention by Colonel Robert G. Ingersoll. the noted orator and agnostic. Ingersoll attempted to reassure the delegates on the moral issue by thundering that the Republicans "do not demand that their candidate shall have a certificate of moral character signed by the Confederate Congress." To illustrate Blaine's courage, Ingersoll christened him (if that is the phrase) with his famous nickname: "Like an armed warrior, like a *plumed knight*, James G. Blaine marched down the halls of the American Congress and threw his shining lance full and fair against the brazen forehead of the defamers of his country and maligners of his honor."

Some observers thought that if the balloting had taken place on the spot, Blaine would have stampeded the convention and received the nomination on the first ballot. Unfortunately for the plumed knight, however, Cincinnati, unlike Washington, did not yet have electric lights, and the supply for the gaslights was cut off suddenly, forcing an adjournment until the next day. One Robert W. Mackey later took credit for this act, but it is more likely that the real villain was Mackey's roommate at the convention, Mr. Matthew Quay. Boss Quay, it would seem, was trusting nothing to Providence in this election either.

In spite of Ingersoll's eloquence, Blaine was stopped, and with the help of Quay and others, a dark horse candidate, Governor Rutherford B. Hayes of Ohio, was nominated on the seventh ballot. One explanation for the choice of Hayes was that he was inoffensive, "a third-rate nonentity, whose only recommendation is that he is obnoxious to no one." This was the view of Henry Adams, a grandson of John Quincy Adams, who attended the convention. When Joseph Pulitzer of the *New York World* was told that in an era of corruption "Hayes had never stolen," Pulitzer replied, "Good God! Has it come to this?"

The Republicans chose William A. Wheeler, by one account a "well-known" congressman from New York, for vice-president. His fame, however, had not spread to Hayes, who whispered to an associate, "Who *is* Wheeler?"

The Democrats met two weeks later and nominated Governer Samuel J. Tilden of New York. In one way the choice was natural enough. The times cried out for reform and Tilden was the most famous reformer in the country, having destroyed the notorious Tweed Ring in New York. As one speaker said, a "reform campaign without Tilden would be like the play of *Hamlet* with Hamlet left out." As no one could imagine this, Tilden was chosen overwhelmingly. In spite of his reputation as a reformer, Tilden seemed a strange choice to many. He was sixty-two years old, in poor health, a rich corporation lawyer and a bachelor ("he never felt the need for a wife"). These were unusual qualifications for a presidential candidate.

In the campaign both sides, of course, called for reform. The Democrats enumerated the scandals of the Grant administration and promised to "throw the rascals out" (a phrase borrowed from Horace Greeley, who had used it four years earlier in his unsuccessful presidential race against Grant).

The Republicans praised their past performances but nev-

"The Two-faced Tilden" (A.B. Frost).

ertheless were intent on improving them. To be on the safe side, they also waved the "bloody flag" of rebellion. Hayes's first order of business was a letter to Blaine, in which he said, "A Democratic victory will bring the Rebellion into power. Our strong ground is the dread of a solid South, *rebel rule*, etc. I hope that you will make these topics prominent in your speeches. *It leads people away from 'hard times,' which is our deadliest foe.*" Blaine was happy to oblige and stumped the country, waving the bloody shirt. A Republican party worker in Indiana summed up the situation in his state: "A

TILDEN.   **HAYES.**

OF THE TWO EVILS
CHOOSE THE LEAST.

Cynicism, 1876 style.

bloody-shirt campaign with money and Indiana is safe." He added that any other type of campaign and no money would be folly.

"Not every Democrat was a Rebel, but every Rebel was a Democrat," reasoned the Republicans. "Is it safe to trust the nation's affairs with men who had once raised their hands against her life?" Ingersoll was more eloquent: "Every man that shot Union soldiers was a Democrat! The man that assassinated Lincoln was a Democrat. Soldiers, every scar you have got on your heroic bodies was given you by a Democrat!" As for Tilden, Ingersoll said he was "a dried-up bachelor, as bad as Buchanan"—a damning charge indeed.

The first returns on the election night indicated that Tilden had won. He had carried New York, Indiana, New Jersey, and Connecticut, as well as the "solid South," giving him an apparent count of 203 electoral votes to 166 for Hayes. "The new era begins," said the Democratic *New York World*. "Peace on earth and to men of good will is the glorious message of this glorious day." The Republican *Indianapolis Journal* sighed, "Tilden is elected. The announcement will carry pain to every loyal heart in the nation, but the inevitable truth may as well be stated." On the morning after the election Hayes wrote his son, conceding defeat, and the following day, James A. Garfield, the Republican leader in the House and a future president, wrote a friend, "It now appears we are defeated by the combined power of rebellion, Catholicism, and whiskey, a trinity very hard to conquer."

Tilden would have been president, too, had it not been for the bumbling of a Democratic state chairman who sent a message to the *New York Times* in the wee hours of the morning after the election, asking for the latest returns. "Please give your estimate of electoral votes secured for Tilden. Answer at once," he said.

Tilden had 184 sure electoral votes and Hayes had 166, but three states with 19 votes—Florida, Louisiana, and South Carolina—were still out, though presumed from early returns to be for Tilden. It didn't take long for the *Times* editor John Reid, a fanatic Republican, to add the 19 doubtful votes to Hayes's total to give him 185 votes and the election. "If they want to know the electoral vote," Reid surmised, "that means they are not certain they have won. If they are still in doubt, then we can go on from here and win the election!" The plot thus was hatched that resulted in stealing the election for Hayes.

Reid awakened the Republican officials and put his plan into action. He telegraphed south, "Hayes is elected if we have carried South Carolina, Florida, and Louisiana. Can you hold your state? Answer immediately." At the same time Republican newspapers announced that "Hayes had 185 electoral votes and is elected."

The *Indianapolis Journal* apologized for its concession statement and noted that "the political situation has undergone a remarkable change. . . . trustworthy advices indicate almost unmistakably that Hayes and Wheeler are elected." Prominent Republicans met with Grant the next morning, and although Grant's first impression was that "it looks to me as if Mr. Tilden was elected," he was prevailed upon to help. Reinforcements were sent to the army in the "disputed" states (troops were already there to police the elections), and "visiting statesmen" were dispatched "to watch the count," since, as Grant said, "The people will not be satisfied unless something is done in regard to it which will look like justice." As a precaution, Republican agents supplied with money were also sent south.

The Democrats were not idle. They had their own "visiting statesmen," as well as men like Thurlow Weed, who offered to buy three of the members of the South Carolina election return board for $30,000. Tilden, however, refused to go along with Weed's plan, believing that "the fiery zealots of the Republican party may try to count me out, but I don't think the better class of Republicans will permit it." Nor did Tilden agree to buy Louisiana or Florida, both of which were offered to him by Republican carpetbagger "recount supervisors," for $200,000 each. (In declining Tilden noted that $200,000 "seemed to be standard.")

Hayes's first reaction to the postelection activity was to scoff. "I think we are defeated in spite of the recent good news," he said. "I am of the opinion that the democrats have carried the country and elected Tilden. . . . I do heartily deprecate these dispatches." As the Republican effort got into high gear, however, he was willing to try. "I don't care for myself," he said. "The party, yes, and the country, too, can stand it; but I care for the poor colored men of the South."

Neither side was blameless in the election practices. As one historian noted, "It is hard to see any difference ethically between marching [illiterate ex-slaves] to the polls with marked ballots [as the Republicans did] and keeping them from voting by threats and intimidation [as the Democrats did]." Another said, "The corruption of one was as heinous as the cruelty of the other."

The issue, however, was not how the votes were cast but who had the most, and thus the Republicans had the job of "going behind the returns" to change the certified Democratic victories in the three states to Republican victories. This they proceeded to do, "not flinching at the task." All the "Returning Boards" were composed of Republicans. In many cases, they simply threw out votes to change the outcome in certain boxes; in other cases they threw out entire boxes. In Precinct 3 of Key West, Florida, for example, in which all the residents were white, the vote was 401 for Tilden against 59 for Hayes. A bottle of ink was spilled on the certificate of the vote on the election night, though, and a new certificate was made the next morning. No allegations of wrongdoing were made, but the box was thrown out on the technicality that the new certificate was not made on the election day.

Money and messages flowed south for five months while the dispute was raging. Furtive communications were exchanged, such as "Hold Florida and you have your own terms," "Be specific about how we will be taken care of," and "Send money. Danger great." Coded telegrams were used, such as "Robinson must go immediately to Philadelphia and then come here," meaning "$3,000 must be deposited in the Centennial Bank in Philadelphia where I can draw it." Other codes were "Doctors plenty," meaning "Returning Board all right," "Cold reports," meaning "situation uncertain," and "South Carolina cotton high absolutely," translated "South Carolina absolutely safe."

As a result of all these shenanigans, two sets of conflicting returns were sent from each of the disputed states, and a constitutional crisis developed. There was a real danger that the inauguration day would arrive without a certified winner. The Senate, which was to announce the vote, was Republican, and the House, which would have to decide an election without a clear winner, was Democratic. "Tilden or Blood!" was heard in many quarters, and one newspaper said, "Tilden has been elected and by the Eternal he shall be inaugurated." The Republicans responded by noting that "General U.S. Grant, not Buchanan, is in charge of affairs at Washington." Grant himself observed that he "did not intend to have two governments or any South American *pronunciamentos.*"

To head off the crisis a number of plans were proposed. A Senate plan called for a commission to settle the dispute. It was to have an equal number of Democrats and Republicans with an additional member chosen by lot from the Senate. Mr. Tilden had some understanding of the laws of probability and realized what the odds were of a Democrat's being chosen by lot from the Republican-dominated Senate. He therefore respectfully declined "to raffle for the Presidency."

Finally the two parties agreed on a commission that would have fifteen members—five from the Senate, five from the House, and five from the Supreme Court. The ten House and Senate members and four of the court members were divided seven to seven between the Democrats and the Republicans. The plan was made acceptable to the Democrats by the specification that the four justices would select the fifth, tacitly understood to be Justice David Davis, who was thought to be friendly to Tilden's cause. As soon as the House passed the bill establishing the commission, however, Davis, in a strange and timely coincidence, was appointed a senator by the Illinois legislature, and the justices subsequently selected Justice Joseph Bradley as the fifteenth member of the commission.

The Democrats still had hopes, for even though Bradley was a Republican (there weren't any other Democratic justices at the time), he had a reputation for independence.

Indeed, the rumor ran that Bradley, on the eve of the decision, had shown his opinion favoring Tilden to the Democratic national chairman. The chairman, however, left Bradley's house too soon. A number of Republican dignitaries spent the rest of the night with the judge.

The next day Bradley sided with the other Republicans on every count, and every disputed state was awarded to Hayes by an eight to seven vote. "It is what I expected," commented Tilden. "Fraud! Dishonesty! Corruption!" was the reaction across the country. "Lead us! We will put you in the White House, where you belong," begged Tilden's supporters.

Hayes was declared elected, but taking his seat was another matter. The country was in an ugly mood and many thought another civil war was imminent. "The judgment in effect exalts fraud, degrades justice, and consigns truth to the dungeon," cried one Democratic senator. "A Louisville editor declared that "100,000 Kentuckians would see that justice was done." It was plain that a deal had to be struck with the South. "If we are saved," said Garfield, "it will be by the rebels."

So it was. Hayes, who had said his only concern was for "the poor colored men of the South," agreed to remove the federal troops from their area, and (his enemies later charged) agreed not to enforce the Fifteenth Amendment that guaranteed their right to vote. The southern Democrats thereupon dropped their objections to Hayes, saying, as Garfield reported, that "they have seen war enough and do not care to follow the lead of their Northern associates, who . . . were invincible in peace and invisible in war."

The deal, made two days before Hayes's inauguration, averted a major crisis. On the inauguration day Hayes's picture was shown in many leading newspapers, labeled with "Fraud!" across his forehead. The *New York Sun* appeared with the same black border it had used to announce the death of Lincoln. Many other papers referred to the new president of the United States as "His Fraudulency," "Old 8 to 7," and simply "Rutherfraud B. Hayes."

Despite the fact that his election was stolen, Hayes was a "good and honest President." He ended reconstruction in the South, weeded grafters out of the government, improved the civil service, and "stood up for the church, the home, and the American gold standard." He is also remembered for his wife, who earned the nickname Lemonade Lucy by banning liquor from the White House. This extreme departure from the Grant era forced the guests to resort to frozen rum punch, concealed in oranges supplied secretly by the servants.

A final touch was put to the 1876 campaign by the cartoonist Thomas Nast in March, 1877. He depicted the Republican elephant bandaged all over, an arm in a sling, holding a crutch, with the caption, "Another such victory and I am undone."

"Another Such Victory and I Am Undone" (Thomas Nast).

MA! MA! WHERE'S MY PA!

The only election to rival the "Log Cabin Campaign" for buffoonery was that of 1884. It had the added distinction of being, by one historical account, "the dirtiest campaign in United States history." According to their enemies, the candidates offered to the electorate were, on the one hand, "the town drunk" and "a coarse debaucher," and on the other, "an unrestrained public plunderer," who "had wallowed in spoils like a rhinoceros in an African pool."

It was the Gilded Age, the era of the robber barons, and a time when Mark Twain said that he could look at a congressman without awe, "even without embarrassment." Another writer said of the times that "the Standard [Oil Company] has done everything with the Pennsylvania legislature except refine it." Against this backdrop it must have taken a special kind of courage—or effrontery—for the chaplain to open the Republican convention with the prayer that "the incoming political campaign may be conducted with that

Blaine as a rhinoceros "wallowing in spoils" (Thomas Nast).

decency, intelligence, patriotism and dignity of temper which become a free and intelligent people."

The Republicans nominated James G. Blaine, of 1876 fame, as their presidential candidate, in a "mass meeting of maniacs" (as the editor of the *Nation* called it). The nomination seriously split the party because of the wide talk of Blaine's "financial irregularities." (Some critics were more direct. In a preconvention cartoon he was labeled "rejected, too crooked.")

A reform group, known as Mugwumps (they had their mugs on one side of the fence and their "Wumps" on the other), refused to support Blaine and bolted to the Democrats. The Blaine Republicans called the Mugwumps "Assistant Democrats" and noted with contempt that they "had their hair parted in the middle, banged in front," and were "neither male nor female."

One of Blaine's enemies was the powerful New York political boss Roscoe Conkling, whose disaffection probably started in 1876 when Blaine referred to him as having a "turkey-gobbler strut" and likened him to "a dunghill." At

"The Presidential Recruiting Office," with Blaine
"rejected, too crooked" (Bernard Gillam).

any rate, when asked if he would support Blaine, Conkling, a
lawyer, replied, "I do not engage in criminal practice."

In contrast to Blaine, the Democratic candidate, Grover
Cleveland, was so honest he was "ugly honest," according to
observers. He subscribed to the well-known but seldom
believed statement that "a public office is a public trust," an
extraordinary view for his time. He was Grover the Good,
and he remained incorruptible throughout his career, to the
surprise and dismay of friends and enemies alike. Even the
1884 campaign did not change him.

In the beginning of the campaign, Cleveland's enemies
could conjure up nothing on him more vile than the charge
that he was a "Presbyterian bigot" and a "cowardly bigot,"
though the terms probably were not meant synonymously.
On the other hand, the Democrats and Mugwumps had a
field day with Blaine's history of shady financial dealings.
Blaine's friends affectionately called him the Plumed Knight
(a name given him in 1876, as already noted, by Robert

"The Tattooed Man"—Blaine's corruption exposed
in a takeoff on a famous painting of the time (Bernard Gillam).

Ingersoll). But to his enemies he was the "tattooed man,"
depicted disrobed in a famous cartoon with "railroad bonds"
and "corruption" written all over his body.

During the campaign a number of compromising letters
regarding Blaine's business deals were discovered and published by the Mugwumps. Among them was one to Warren
Fisher, a business associate, which was particularly damning. In it Blaine asked for a special favor and concluded with
"Kind regards to Mrs. Fisher. Burn this letter." The Democrats now sang and chanted:

> *Burn this letter! Burn this letter!*
> *Kind regards to Mrs. Fisher.*

To the Republican rhyme,

> *Blaine! Blaine! The man from Maine!*

they answered:

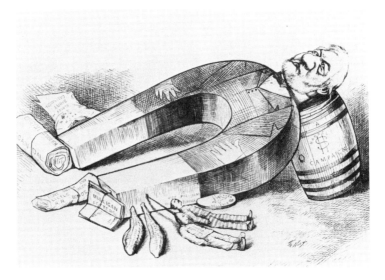

"Blaine, the Magnetic Statesman" attracts corruption
(Thomas Nast).

Blaine! Blaine! James G. Blaine!
The continental liar from the state of Maine.
Burn this letter!

The Republicans counterattacked by calling Cleveland a
"lecherous beast," an "obese nincompoop," a "drunken sot,"
and in reference to his 250-pound bulk, "a small man everywhere except on the hay scales." Because as governor of New
York he had not prevented the execution of two murderers,
he was also dubbed "the hangman of Buffalo."

The worst for Cleveland, however, was yet to come. Ten
days after the Democratic convention adjourned, the *Buffalo Telegraph* published an article with the front-page
headline, "A *Terrible* Tale: A Dark Chapter in a Public
Man's History," and the subtitle, "The Pitiful Story of Maria
Halphin and Governor Cleveland's Son." Then followed the
facts that Cleveland had had an illicit affair with the thirty-
six-year-old widow Mrs. Halphin, who had subsequently

borne a child. For good measure the *Telegraph* added that
Cleveland was a drunkard and a libertine who had no business running for president.

The Republicans were exuberant, and the Democrats
were dismayed. What were they to do? they asked of Cleveland. "Whatever you do," he said, with characteristic honesty, "tell the truth." The truth, Cleveland said, was that he
had had an affair with Mrs. Halphin eight years earlier and
that although he was not sure of the child's paternity, he had
contributed to its support. The boy was now growing up with
adoptive parents. Mrs. Halphin was out of the public eye
and refused to make any statements.

"Another Voice for Cleveland" (Frank Beard in *Judge*).

Ministers and reporters, however, made statements aplenty. Typical was the *New York Sun* article that read, "We do not believe that the American people will knowingly elect to the Presidency a coarse debauchee who would bring his harlots with him to Washington and hire lodgings for them convenient to the White House." Republican cartoons showed an infant labeled "one more vote for Cleveland." Paraders chanted, "Ma, Ma, where's my pa?" to which the Democrats replied, "Gone to the White House. Ha! Ha! Ha!" The Reverend George Bull of Buffalo declaimed, "The issue is evidently not between the two parties, but between the brothel and the home, between lust and law." Cleveland was a regular Casanova, it seemed, for as the good reverend went on to say, "Investigations now disclose still more proof of debaucheries too horrible to relate and too vile to be readily believed. Women now married and anxious to cover the sins of their youth have been his victims, and are now alarmed lest their relations with him be exposed." The Reverend Henry Ward Beecher, however, defended Cleveland, accusing Blaine of "awhoring after votes." He said he would support Cleveland and that if every New Yorker who had violated the Seventh Commandment also voted for him, he would carry the state by 200,000 votes.

Fortunately for Cleveland the Halphin affair broke early in the campaign. There was time for the voters to put it in proper perspective. Many agreed with the Mugwump who observed that Cleveland had great integrity in office but questionable credentials in private life, whereas Blaine was a model husband and father but was delinquent in office. He said therefore, "We should elect Mr. Cleveland to the public office which he is so qualified to fill and retire Mr. Blaine to the private life which he is so admirably fitted to adorn."

With a week left to go in the campaign, Blaine appeared to have a definite edge. This seemed to prove that charges of stealing went down more easily with the voters than those of drunkenness and illicit sex. In the last week, however, two events in one day destroyed Blaine.

The first blow was dealt to him in the afternoon by a preacher, who while trying to help inadvertently proved to be Blaine's undoing. The occasion was a gathering of Protestant clergymen in New York who had endorsed Blaine, and the speaker was the Reverend Dr. Samuel Burchard. At one point in his rambling speech the Reverend Dr. Burchard assured Blaine that the clergy were with him and that he and his colleagues would never support any candidate of the party of "rum, Romanism, and rebellion." New Yorkers didn't mind candidates running against rebels (after all, they had been doing it for twenty years), nor did they object, at least at that time, to swipes at drunks, such as they imagined Cleveland to be. But the Catholics among them did not take kindly to the slur against their religion. Poor Blaine was not really listening and thus did not repudiate the remark, thereby allowing the Democrats to make it seem that he agreed with the preacher. No one, in fact, seemed to notice the remark when it was made except a Democratic spy, who rushed to Democratic headquarters with the incredibly good news. "Surely Blaine met this remark," someone said. "That is the astounding thing," said the observer. "He made no reference to the words."

Overnight the Democrats printed handbills with "Rum, Romanism, and Rebellion," in bold letters and distributed them in every Catholic neighborhood in New York City. The handbills shamelessly implied that Blaine had approved the remark by his silence, and as usual in such cases, the impression grew that Blaine had made the remark himself. Blaine issued a disclaimer three days later, but the damage was done.

The second fateful event of that day was a dinner at Delmonico's Restaurant held for Blaine by a group of his wealthy supporters, including Jay Gould, John Jacob Astor, and Cyrus W. Field. The next morning the newspapers carried scathing editorial comments on the gathering, with front-page headlines like "*THE ROYAL FEAST OF BEL-SHAZZAR BLAINE AND THE MONEY KINGS.*" A front-page cartoon showed Blaine and the millionaires at a table laden with terrapin, canvasback duck, and champagne, with a hungry family in the foreground begging for crumbs. The day, as the *The New World* reported, was "Mr. Blaine's black Wednesday."

As if all this weren't enough for Blaine, Providence sent a driving rain down on upstate New York on the election day,

"Belshazzar" Blaine flanked by the money kings
(W.H. McDougall in the *New York World*).

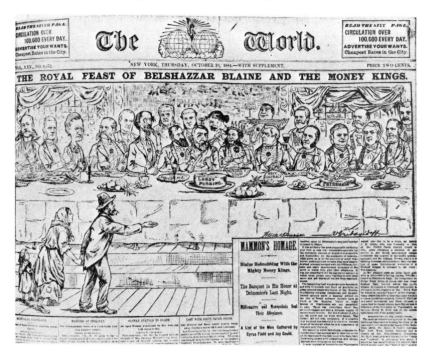

which sharply reduced the Republican vote. Blaine lost New York by 1,149 votes, and with it the election. Outside New York the candidates virtually were tied (Cleveland, 183 electoral votes, and Blaine, 182), and so New York's 36 votes determined the outcome.

Because of the rains and the Reverend Dr. Burchard, Blaine later attributed his defeat to the fact that "the Lord sent upon us an ass in the shape of a preacher, and a rainstorm to lessen our vote in New York." Four years later the memory of Dr. Burchard still lingered in Republican circles. Their candidate, Benjamin Harrison, grandson of our friend William Henry Harrison of 1840, refused to leave his home during the campaign. "I have a great risk of meeting a fool at home," he said, "but the candidate who travels cannot escape him."

The irony of the dirty campaign of 1884 perhaps is that the candidate with the reputation for shady dealing and dirty tricks was done in by his supporters, Providence, and a dirty trick of his opposition.

THE BULL MOOSE CAMPAIGN

In America in 1912 the automobile self-starter was introduced, suffragettes marched on New York's Fifth Avenue, hard liquor was selling at six quarts for one dollar, Model T Fords abounded on the roads, there was no personal income tax, and the national debt stood at just eleven dollars per person. The year's best selling novel was Zane Grey's *Riders of the Purple Sage*, and the popular songs were "Moonlight Bay," "Waiting for the Robert E. Lee," and Irving Berlin's "When the Midnight Choo Choo Leaves for Alabam." Sarah Bernhardt was starring in *Queen Elizabeth*, the first feature-length motion picture shown in America; the Boston Red Sox moved into newly completed Fenway Park; the Indian head/buffalo nickel was issued; a heart attack was first diagnosed in a living patient; and the fourth down was added to football. It was also the year the *Titanic* went down and the year of an unmatched presidential campaign, which saw a sitting president, a past president, and a future president in a three-way battle for the White House.

The incumbent president was Republican William Howard Taft, his challenger from within his party was ex-president Theodore Roosevelt, and the future president was Democrat Woodrow Wilson. In the language of the campaign, however, the race was between a "rat," "the most cunning and adroit demagogue that modern civilization had produced since Napoleon III," and a "long-haired bookworm of a professor."

The most colorful of the three contenders was Teddy Roosevelt, who to the dismay of Senator Mark Hanna had become president upon the assassination of President William McKinley in 1901. "I told McKinley it was a mistake to nominate that wild man," said Hanna. "Now look! That damned cowboy is President of the Unites States!"

Roosevelt had used the presidency as a "bully pulpit" and lashed out at the trusts and the "malefactors of great wealth." His motto was "Speak softly and carry a big stick," and he wielded his big stick freely. As he said of the building of the Panama Canal, for example, "I took the Isthmus, started the Canal, and then left Congress—not to debate the Canal, but to debate me." He was an exciting president and one of the few who seemed to relish the job. "No President has ever enjoyed himself as much as I have enjoyed myself," he said, on leaving the office in 1909.

Roosevelt had been elected to his second term in 1904, the only successful Republican candidate since Lincoln who was not a Civil War army officer born in Ohio. But on the election night, after the results were in, Roosevelt made one of his few political mistakes. He said, "The wise custom which limits the President to two terms regards the substance and not the form, and under no circumstances will I be a candidate for or accept another nomination." He later admitted, "I would cut off my hand [at the wrist] . . . if I could recall that written statement."

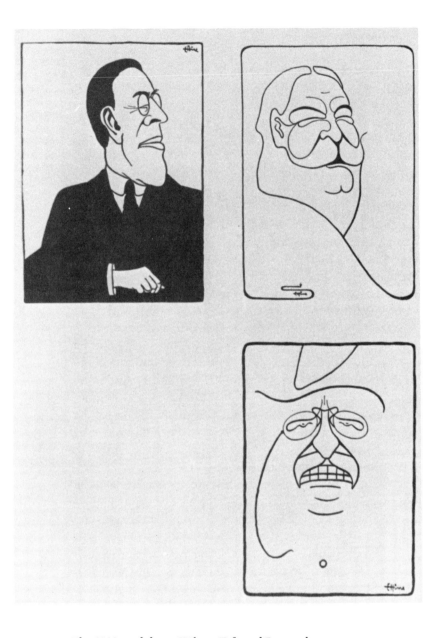

The 1912 candidates, Wilson, Taft, and Roosevelt
(E. Hine; CULVER PICTURES).

In contrast to Teddy Roosevelt, Taft did not enjoy the presidency. "I have come to the conclusion," he once said, "that the major work of the President is to increase the gate receipts of expositions and fairs and bring tourists to town." When Roosevelt decided to make Taft his successor, he teased him by saying, "I have clairvoyant powers. I see a man standing before me weighing about three-hundred-and-fifty pounds. There is something hanging over his head. . . . At one time it looks like the presidency—then again it looks like the chief justiceship." "Make it the Presidency," cried Mrs. Taft. "Make it the chief justiceship," said Taft.

At 330 pounds, Taft was the heaviest of all the presidents, and his weight was the butt of many jokes. A Supreme Court justice said that Taft was the politest man alive. "I heard that recently he rose in a streetcar and gave his seat to three women." One observer said, in criticizing his presidency, that Taft was "a large body surrounded by men who knew exactly what they wanted."

Despite the jokes about him and his reluctance to be president, Taft was elected in 1908 with Roosevelt's help. On the inauguration day Washington experienced one of the nastiest blizzards in its history, prompting Taft to say to Roosevelt, "I always said it would be a cold day when I got to be President of the United States."

The third candidate of 1912, Woodrow Wilson, had his first experience in politics in 1860. "I was," Wilson said, "standing at my father's gateway . . . when I was four years old, and [heard] someone pass and say that Mr. Lincoln was elected and there was to be war." Wilson's first love was politics, but he took his doctorate and by 1890 had settled down to a professor's life at Princeton. When he finally decided to take up politics, his rise was "the phenomenon of all history." In September, 1910, he was a college president who had never held a public office, and on March 4, 1913, he was president of the United States.

Taft as Teddy Roosevelt's heir apparent in happier times
(Joseph Klepper; CULVER PICTURES).

Roosevelt was only fifty years old when he turned over the presidency to Taft. He was at the height of his popularity and could easily have had the third term that he so badly wanted if it had not been for his rash promise not to run again. To drown his sorrows at leaving office, he plunged into the rough-and-tumble life of the outdoors. By 1910, however, he was having second thoughts about Taft. Either Roosevelt was getting the "itch to run again" himself, as his foes suggested, or he genuinely thought Taft was a mistake. "Mistake, hell! He was a disaster," said an editor who was friendly to Teddy.

The contenders, featuring Roosevelt as a thorn in Taft's flesh
(Clifford Berryman; Library of Congress).

Taft was at a loss to understand Roosevelt's increasing
hostility toward him. He had tried to please Teddy in everything he did and indeed to keep himself in Roosevelt's
shadow. "When someone addresses Taft as 'Mr. President,' "

one wag said, "he instinctively turns around to see where Roosevelt is." Nevertheless, relations between the two continued to deteriorate, and finally, upon his return from an African big-game hunt in 1912, Roosevelt announced his candidacy, coining the expression, "My hat's in the ring." He added, "The fight is on and I'm stripped to the buff." He explained that his earlier promise not to seek a third term meant no third *consecutive* term.

At first Taft was genuinely grieved at Roosevelt's break with him. "Roosevelt was my closest friend," he said sorrowfully. But as Roosevelt continued to attack him as "disloyal" and guilty of "the grossest and most astounding hypocrisy," he decided that he had reached his limit. "I have been a man of straw long enough," Taft told the *New York Times*. "Even a rat in a corner will fight!"

"Forward!"—The Roosevelt-Taft spilt (CULVER PICTURES).

Taft controlled the party machinery, but in 1912 presidential primaries were being held for the first time in history, and Roosevelt used them to get delegates. By then Taft was resolved to keep Roosevelt from ever becoming president again, and he fought hard in the primaries. But a president who had called himself "a man of straw" and had compared himself to "a cornered rat" could not arouse the enthusiasm of the voters. This was especially true when he had an opponent like Roosevelt, who kept reminding the voters that Taft was not only a "rat in a corner," but a fat, sweating one at that. For good measure, Teddy added that Taft was a hypocrite, a promoter of fraud, an ingrate who would bite the hand that fed him, and a man "with brains of about three guinea-pig power." The results were predictable. Roosevelt won 278 delegates in the primaries to Taft's 48.

The nomination, however, was another matter. The Republican convention was held in Chicago on June 18, but the nomination was decided before the delegates convened. The national committee was dominated by Taft men, and it ruled on the seating of the delegates. In one credentials fight after another the committee ruled in favor of Taft. "There is no form of rascality which the Taft men have not resorted to," thundered Teddy to the press, but it did no good. When the convention opened, Taft had 566 delegates—only 540 were needed for nomination—and Roosevelt had 466.

To counter what he called the "steam-roller" tactics of the Taft men—using another term coined in 1912—Roosevelt personally came to the convention. "It is a fight against theft—and the thieves will not win," he roared. Newspapermen asked: Was he set for a tough fight? Did he welcome it? Was he in shape for it? "I feel fine," Teddy said, "I'm feeling like a bull moose!" Thus the name of the campaign was determined.

On one vote after another the Taft delegates were seated at the convention while the Bull Moosers whistled "Toot,

Toot!" and rubbed sandpaper together in imitation of the sounds of a steamroller. "We stand at Armageddon, and we battle for the Lord," screamed Roosevelt. In spite of the "stolen" delegates, the issue was in doubt until the end. Taft's men said they had a majority of forty, and Roosevelt's men said they had a majority of forty. What did it mean? "It means," chortled a senator, "that there are at least eighty liars in the convention."

Warren G. Harding gave the nomination speech for Taft, calling him "the greatest progressive of the age," which must have infuriated Roosevelt. Harding droned on that Taft "was the finest example of lofty principles since the immortal Lincoln bore the scourge of vengeful tongues without a murmur from his noble heart."

When Harding's speech finally was over, the voting began. By this time it was clear that Taft would win, and so Teddy instructed his delegates not to participate. The result of the first ballot was Taft, 561 (enough to win), Roosevelt, 107, and 344 "present and not voting." The verdict announced to a reporter was, "The only question now is which corpse gets the flowers." "Chicago is a bad place to steal in," warned Teddy.

The Democratic convention was held a week later in Baltimore. A big question was: Would William Jennings Bryan be a candidate? "While life lasts," was the answer given by one of his "admirers."

The two chief contenders were Senator Champ Clark of Missouri and Woodrow Wilson, who had moved from the groves of academe to the governorship of New Jersey. Clark was ridiculed as the "patent medicine man," because for some reason he had signed a testimonial for Electric Bitters, saying, "It seemed that all the organs in my body were out of order, but three bottles of Electric Bitters made me all right." He was also made fun of for the song his followers sang at rallies—the old "houn' dawg" song with the chorus:

> *"I doan' keer if he is a houn',*
> *You gotta quit kickin' my dawg aroun!"*

Wilson was a "long-haired professor" with no business in politics. Not much more seemed necessary to add.

The *New York World* "had hoped that it would not be necessary to treat Mr. Clark's candidacy seriously. That was a compliment we paid to the intelligence of western and southern Democrats, but it was a compliment which we now find was undeserved." As ballot after ballot was taken, however, it was decided that Mr. Clark *was* a serious candidate, since he led by increasing margins on every ballot. On the tenth ballot, thanks to ninety votes from New York, Champ had a majority. Two-thirds of the delegates were necessary for nomination, but no candidate who reached a majority had ever failed to go on to the nomination.

At this point Bryan changed his vote from Clark to Wilson on the grounds that New York's vote for Clark proved Clark was not a progressive. Some said it proved Clark might win before a deadlock could develop to result in Bryan's nomination. This slowed the Clark bandwagon somewhat, but it still took thirty-six more ballots to defeat him. Wilson was chosen on the forty-sixth ballot. It was predestination, said the Presbyterian Wilson. "God ordained that I should be the next President of the United States," he said to his astonished party chairman, who had expected to get some credit for it himself.

The convention selected to run for vice-president Governor Thomas R. Marshall of Indiana. Marshall's fame rests on his assertion that "what this country needs is a really good five-cent cigar."

Roosevelt and his group, calling themselves the Progressive party, held their convention in August. Roosevelt was nominated, to no one's surprise, and in his acceptance speech he declared that 1912 was the year in which the people had their chance to destroy the "rotting husks," otherwise known as the Republican and Democratic parties. The Democrats, he had said earlier, were "as stupid, bourbon and reactionary as ever before," and as for Taft, his "nomination was fraudulent." To suggestions that the Progressives compromise with the Republicans to keep out the hated Democrats, Teddy replied, "I hold that Mr. Taft stole the nomination, and I do not feel like arbitrating with a pickpocket as to whether or not he shall keep my watch."

One cynic said the Bull Moose platform was "Roosevelt's Confession of Faith," and another said it contained everything "from the shorter catechism to how to build a birchbark canoe." The *New York Times* sneered that the platform was a socialist document and sympathized with poor Eugene Debs, the candidate of still another party—the Socialists—who after the Progressive raid had only "one university professor hereabout" still faithful to his cause.

The issues in the campaign were the big trusts and the high cost of living. Beef had not been so expensive in thirty years. At seventeen cents per pound, it was difficult for the average worker to buy, with wages at two dollars per day. The Republicans promised the full dinner pail and the Democrats promised tariff reform and new labor laws. Taft campaigned very little, figuring that although he could not win he could keep Roosevelt from winning, which was his greatest hope. He was sorry that the Democrats, "an incompetent group," would win, "but the fear of Mr. Roosevelt's success made it necessary" to campaign. Wilson and Roosevelt campaigned vigorously, each considering the other his major opponent. Roosevelt knew he could beat Taft but was not sure about Wilson. Thus his speeches, according to the *New York Evening Post*, were like those "Custer might have made to his scouts when he saw the Indians coming." Wilson pretended to take little notice of the Taft-Roosevelt feud,

"An Irresistible Force Meets an Immovable Object"
(Joseph Keppler; CULVER PICTURES).

preferring, he said, the strategy of Napoleon: "Don't interfere when your enemy is destroying himself."

In spite of Wilson's having called Bryan a "demagogue" in 1908 and wishing "that we could do something, at once dignified and effective, to knock Mr. Bryan once and for all into a cocked hat," Bryan was willing to campaign for the Democrats. This he did, as unstintingly as he had for himself, speaking ten times per day for seven weeks. One true charge he hurled at Roosevelt was that Teddy had stolen his Bull Moose ideas from the Democrats. "So I have," Roosevelt replied. "That is quite true. I have taken every one of them except those suited for the inmates of lunatic asylums."

What little campaigning Taft did was largely aimed at Roosevelt. He called him a "fakir," a "juggler," a "green goods man," and a "gold brickman," and he said that by manipulation and deceit, "He is seeking to make his followers 'Holy Rollers.'" To his wife, however, Taft said, "Sometimes I think I might as well give up. . . . There are so many people in the country who don't like me . . . apparently on the Dr. Fell principle:

> '*I don't like you, Dr. Fell,*
> *The reason why I cannot tell,*
> *But this I know and know full well,*
> *I don't like you, Dr. Fell.*"

Taft never liked campaigning and knew he was not good at it. The closest he ever came to complaining at having to do it, however, was when he marveled to an aide about how well McKinley campaigned. "He was a born undertaker," said Taft.

Roosevelt fired much of his ammunition at Taft, as when, for example, he noted several Taft badges in a crowd and observed that "they are the appropriate color of yellow." Taft's supporters replied in kind, with Harding comparing Roosevelt inevitably to Benedict Arnold and saying that he was "utterly without conscience and truth, and the greatest faker of all time." Another Taft supporter said of Roosevelt, "I wish I could believe he intended to do a single honest thing . . . if he were to be elected. I cannot." Still another characterized Roosevelt as "as sweet a gentleman as ever scuttled a ship or cut a throat."

Wilson and Roosevelt also had a few choice words for each other. To Roosevelt's suggestion that Wilson should belong to his Ananias Club (named for a biblical character who was put to death for lying), Wilson countered that Roosevelt was a "self-appointed divinity," who had talked a good game of trust-busting but had done nothing when he was president. "There is no man who is big enough to play Providence," added Wilson, with the tone of one who knew.

Even Debs joined the assault on Roosevelt, chiding him for never having spent "a day in jail." Neither Roosevelt nor any of the others, continued Debs, had ever been hit on the head by a policeman or had produced enough "to feed a gallinipper" (a large mosquito). Because Debs had had these experiences, his reasoning went, he could relate to working people. (Wilson would later help him relive these experiences by jailing him during World War I for the "treasonable acts" of criticizing Wilson's administration. Debs, however, was not deterred. He conducted his next campaign from his jail cell.)

Toward the end of the campaign there was a flash of drama when an anti-third-term fanatic shot Roosevelt just before he was to deliver a speech. Physicians wanted to send him to a hospital, but Roosevelt said, "I'll make this speech or die; one or the other."

"There is a bullet in my body," he said to the astonished audience. "But it is nothing.... It takes more than that to kill a Bull Moose!" After the speech he was rushed to the hospital, where it was discovered that the bullet had struck his metal spectacles case, which prevented it from going more than four inches into his chest wall and thus saved his life.

Wilson and Taft both sent telegrams of admiration and sympathy and suspended their campaigns while Roosevelt was in the hospital. In six days Teddy was back on the hustings, to the amazement of his doctors, and the campaign went on.

On October 30, toward the end of the campaign, Taft's running mate, Vice President Sherman, died, and an arrangement had to be made in case the Taft ticket received any electoral votes. Nicholas Murray Butler, the president of Columbia University, was asked to take Sherman's place on the ticket, and he agreed, "as long as there is no chance of my being elected Vice President."

The election results were 6,296,547 votes for Wilson, 4,126,020 for Roosevelt, and 3,486,720 for Taft. The electoral vote was a landslide victory for Wilson, who received 435 votes, to 88 for Roosevelt and 8 for Taft.

End of the Bull Moose Party
(Edward W. Kemble; CULVER PICTURES).

The Taft cow Pauline grazing on the lawn
of the State, War and Navy Building
(Library of Congress).

Roosevelt said, "The fight is over. We are beaten. There is only one thing to do and that is go back to the Republican party. You can't hold a party like the Progressive party together.... There are no loaves and fishes."

Taft was pleased with the outcome. He was out of the White House, which he hated, and Roosevelt was not in it. Taft, a good and honest man, will be remembered as a good Supreme Court chief justice and as the last president to keep a cow in Washington.

Wilson went on to greatness as the nation's leader in World War I. He also brought the country an eight-hour working day, workmen's compensation, and the anti-child-labor law. He was the first successful candidate to stump openly (as we know it) for himself. He proved that a candidate could travel, shake hands, speak across the country, and still retain his dignity. He was also an idealist with vision, which as one historian has said is the reason Wilson's name still appears in the speeches of Democratic candidates, although no Republican has mentioned Taft for fifty years.

★ ★ ★ 9 ★ ★ ★

HOOVER AND AL

The election of 1928 was the last one in the Roaring Twenties, one of the most exciting eras of American history. Daring young flappers shocked their elders with their short skirts, bobbed hair, and free use of cosmetics and cigarettes. People flocked to hear the jazz bands play such tunes as "Yes, We Have No Bananas" and idolized such heroes as Charles A. Lindbergh, Rudolph Valentino, and Babe Ruth. In 1928 Henry Ford unveiled his new Model A, speculation soared in the bull market where stocks had reached a "permanently high plateau," and because of prohibition, illegal drinking clubs, called speakeasies, were filled to capacity. Added to all this was one of our most colorful presidential elections, in which the main contestants were a mining engineer who was also a millionaire and a "dry" on prohibition, versus an unabashed "wet" Roman Catholic from the "sidewalks of New York."

The outgoing president was Calvin Coolidge, who was, in the words of the defense attorney Clarence Darrow, "the greatest man ever to come out of Plymouth Notch, Vermont," and who "looked like he had been weaned on a pickle," in the opinion of Alice Roosevelt Longworth, Teddy's daughter. Coolidge had assumed the presidency upon Harding's death in 1923 and was elected in his own right in 1924. There was almost as much speculation among his fellow Republican hopefuls about Coolidge's plans for 1928 as there was in the stock market itself, but on August 3, 1927, Silent Cal tried to relieve the tension with the wordy (for him) statement: "I do not choose to run for President in 1928."

Ordinarily this simple declaration should have settled the issue, but since it was a political statement, everyone wondered if it meant that Coolidge *did* choose to run. Herbert Hoover, the leading party hopeful, and "a fat Coolidge," according to the noted writer H. L. Mencken, looked up the word choose in the dictionary to see if it had any colloquial meaning peculiar to Vermont. Meanwhile Senator Charles Curtis, another hopeful, asked Coolidge for amplification, which, of course, he never got. Everyone would have known that Coolidge was serious if they had heard Mrs. Coolidge's remark, "Papa says there's going to be a depression."

Hoover finally decided to bring the matter to a head. He asked Coolidge directly if he meant to file in the Ohio primary. No, said Coolidge. Would he mind if Hoover filed? Why not? said Coolidge. Some months later, Hoover, still uncertain, offered Coolidge the 400 convention delegates he had accumulated, to which Coolidge replied, "If you have four-hundred delegates, you better keep them."

Prospects for victory never looked better for Republican hopefuls, if they could get rid of Coolidge. Money was gushing from the factories and pouring from the assembly lines, and "God was in His Heaven," as Mark Hanna said of McKinley's better days. The only cloud on the horizon was farm prices, which curiously had slumped while industry

Hoover with his collar, a trademark of the caricaturists
(United Press International Photo).

was booming. To allay any fears on this score, however, Coolidge explained, "Well, farmers never have made money."

The Republican convention opened in Kansas City on June 12, with Coolidge's status still up in the air. The odds-on favorite, assuming no Coolidge candidacy, was Hoover, or "wonder boy," as Coolidge referred to him in private. The keynote address was long and so filled with praise that the humorist Will Rogers thought the speaker "was referring to Our Savior, till they told me, 'No, it was Coolidge.' " Will added, "The way he rated 'em was Coolidge, The Lord, and then Lincoln."

There was at first a "Draft Coolidge" movement, which caused Mark Hanna's daughter to proclaim, "Hoover is done. That much is certain." This was followed by a demonstration by the farmers, who were pushing "anyone but Hoover." William Green, president of the American federation of Labor, who was in town, called for 2.75 percent beer for the workingman and a five-day week, in that order, and outside the convention hall Kansas City authorities raided four bootlegging establishments.

In the end order prevailed, the "Draft Coolidge" movement died, and Hoover was nominated. For vice-president the convention chose Curtis, who was to be the first Osage Indian in that exalted position. On the selection of Curtis, Will Rogers said, "The Republican party owed Curtis something, but I didn't think they would be so low down as to pay him that way." Will had alerted the delegates earlier that "Dawes [Coolidge's vice-president] is flying here to keep them from sentencing him to another four years."

In Hoover's acceptance speech he told the nation: "We in America are nearer the final triumph over poverty than ever before in the history of any land. . . . The poorhouse is vanishing from among us." As to the burning issue in the campaign, Hoover had written earlier to "dry" Senator Borah

that prohibition was "a great social and economic experiment, noble in motive and far-reaching in purpose." Thus
Hoover seemed to be "dry," but he "was quiet about it." The
"wets," however, shortened his description to Borah to "the
noble experiment" and used it against him in the big cities.
They kept quiet in the rural areas, which "would vote dry as
long as the voters could stagger to the polls."

The Democratic convention opened in Houston on June
26, and there was never any doubt that the candidate would
be "wet" Governor Al Smith, or Al(cohol) Smith, of New
York. His name was put up for the nomination by Franklin
D. Roosevelt, who concluded his address with: "We offer
one who has the will to win—who not only deserves success
but commands it. Victory is his habit—the happy warrior,
Alfred Smith." Roosevelt had nominated Al twice before—
in 1920 and in 1924—which moved Will Rogers to say,
"Franklin Roosevelt, a fine and wonderful man, who has
devoted his life to nominating Al Smith, did his act from
memory." He added, "You could wake him in the middle of
the night and he would start to nominate Al."

Al was a proven vote getter and a formidable campaigner,
but he had formidable drawbacks as well, especially in rural,
smalltown America. First of all he was "wet," which many
thought was enough to damn him to hell. In addition he was
a product of Tammany Hall, a city slicker from New York,
and a Roman Catholic. Not even one of these characteristics
had ever been found in a candidate for president, let alone all
three! Teddy Roosevelt was the previous candidate nearest
to a big-city man, and he got around this by proclaiming
himself a rancher.

The Democratic platform was not "wet," but it would have
been difficult to say that the platform was "dry." It pledged
"the party and its nominees to an honest effort to support the
Eighteenth Amendment [prohibition] and all other provisions of the federal Constitution and all laws enacted pur-

suant thereto." Smith, saying, with candor reminiscent of John Quincy Adams's, that he would as soon lose "as stand for something I don't believe in," immediately sent a telegram to the convention outlining his views. The telegram called for "fundamental changes in the present provisions for national prohibition" and arrived just as the convention was adjourning, which probably was just as well for Al.

"The Sniper" (© 1928 by the *New York Times* Company. Reprinted by permission).

THE SNIPER.

The official campaign followed standard lines. The issue, as the Republicans put it, was "Hoover and Happiness or Smith and Soup Houses? Which Shall It Be?" They promised "a chicken in every pot and two cars in every garage." Hoover said, "The slogan of progress is changing from the full dinner pail [McKinley's 1896 slogan] to the full garage." Republican cartoonists showed Al advocating "the full beer bucket." "The Republican Party," read an ad, "isn't a *Poor Man's Party*. Republican prosperity has erased that degrading word from our political vocabulary." Another slogan was "Let's keep what we've got. Prosperity didn't just happen."

The Democrats referred to Hoover as humorless and dull and repeated the Republicans' own preconvention jokes about him. "He smokes grimly," one said, which probably was funny to those who had seen him try. "Hoover asked someone to lend him a nickel," said another, "to buy a soda for a friend. 'Here's a dime,' was the reply. 'Treat them all.' "

To call attention to Hoover's long stay in England before joining the Coolidge administration and the pro-British labeling he subsequently received, the Democrats composed the song:

> *O 'Erbert lived over the h'ocean.*
> *O 'Erbert lived over the sea;*
> *O 'oo will go down to the h'ocean,*
> *And drown 'Erbert 'Oover for me?*

Both candidates used the radio extensively, gave stump speeches, and rode in motor cavalcades. Charles Lindbergh endorsed Hoover. Babe Ruth was publicly for Smith. Al even appeared on television, becoming the first candidate to do so. His acceptance speech at Albany was broadcast by General Electric to its Schenectady plant fifteen miles away. The television set was described as a "strange, box-like contraption with a lens on front."

The unofficial campaign was vicious on the issues of pro-hibition and Smith's religion. The Ku Klux Klan did not build bunkers along the coast to keep the pope out, as Mencken suggested they would, but they did everything else they could think of. One example of their work was the publication of a bogus "Knights of Columbus Oath," which pledged priests to "wage war on Protestants and Masons" and to flay, lay waste, burn, poison, and so on.

Countless ministers did their moral and religious duties, too. In New York the Reverend John Roach Straton insisted that the Democrats, with Smith, had made "a covenant with death" and were "in agreement with hell." The Reverend Mordecai Ham told his flock in Oklahoma, "If you vote for Al Smith, you're voting against Christ and you'll all be damned."

"A vote for Smith is a vote for the Pope" was a tenet of faith with many voters. A typical flier showed Al at the opening of the new Holland Tunnel joining Manhattan and New Jersey, with a caption stating that if elected, Smith would extend the tunnel under the Atlantic Ocean to the Vatican's basement. A more realistic fear was that the pope would come by train, as an Indiana Klansman warned. "Watch the trains!" he cried. "The Pope may arrive in person on the north-bound train tomorrow!" A crowd gathered but was disappointed.

A Republican committeewoman in Virginia wrote a widely circulated letter stating that "Mr. Hoover, himself, and the National Committee are depending on the women to save our country . . . from being Romanized and rum-ridden." Hoover repudiated the letter immediately, saying that it "did violence to every instinct I possess." For the most part, however, Hoover wisely ignored the religious issue and the "political parsons."

On the lighter side, Al was accused of being a drunk, who required "two persons to hold him up" wherever he went. He was also called a Socialist, a charge that angered the Socialist candidate Norman Thomas, who didn't think Al deserved such praise. Finally, one well-known columnist alleged that Al's legislative record showed that he "favored prostitution as well as the saloon." The writer later admitted he was wrong and retracted the charge, because "a debate on the subject of harlotry was not worthy of a Presidential campaign." This praise and damnation attack caused another newsman to say, "None of the rest of us can put so much poison into a libel as he [Al's attacker] manages to leave in a retraction."

In one particularly hectic campaign rally at which the Happy Warrior was speaking, a heckler shouted, "Tell us all you know, Al. It won't take long." Al's quick retort was, "I'll tell us all we both know. It won't take any longer."

Smith was the best performer on the stump that the Democrats had ever had, with the possible exception of Bryan, and he gave his enemies hell in a manner that would not be seen again for twenty years. "Pour it on 'em Al, pour it on 'em!" responded his partisans.

A favorite gambit of Al's was to read and comment publicly on the Republican campaign literature. "Here's a good one for you," he would say. " 'Republican efficiency has filled the workingman's dinner pail and his gasoline tank besides, and placed the whole nation in the silk stocking class!' Now just draw on your imagination for a moment, and see if you can in your mind's eye picture a man working at seventeen-fifty a week going out to a chicken dinner in his own automobile with silk socks on."

Mercifully the campaign finally ended. Hoover got over 21-million votes to Smith's 16 million and won the electoral vote by a margin of 444 to 87. Al was beaten decisively, but he polled the largest vote any Democratic candidate had ever received, twice as many as his party had gotten in 1924. Al also carried the nation's twelve largest cities, building the foundation for the great Democratic majorities of the next twenty years.

"A Bird in the Hand . . . ," the GOP with the full dinner pail,
and Al with his full beer bucket (Jay N. "Ding" Darling;
courtesy of The University Libraries, The University of Iowa).

His enemies could quip that after the election Al sent a
one-word cable to the pope: "Unpack"; but Al Smith had no
reason to hang his head. Indeed in one way he was lucky and
the last laugh was on Hoover. As the columnist Elmer Davis
said, "Adult Americans elected [Hoover] for the same reason

that would have led Americans under the age of 10 to elect Santa Claus." But Santa Claus never came. Instead there was the stock market crash of 1929 and the Great Depression, and Calvin Coolidge was proved right for saying that when "people are thrown out of work, unemployment results." Herbert Hoover, a good and honest man, has had his name linked with hardship and disaster ever since. His bad luck was summed up by Coolidge: "If you put a rose in Hoover's hand, it would wilt."

★ ★ 10 ★ ★

THE ONLY THIRD TERM

The election of 1940, like that of 1860, was fought under the cloud of war. Europe was ablaze with World War II, France had fallen, and England stood alone against the madman Adolf Hitler. In America, Joe DiMaggio's batting average "slipped" to .352 and the Yankees lost the pennant for the first time in five years. The first Social Security checks went out, the first nylon stockings went on sale, and the first McDonald's hamburger stand opened in a drive-in theater in Pasadena, California. Two best-selling books were *For Whom the Bell Tolls* and *You Can't Go Home Again*, and Gene Autry was popularizing his new song, "Back in the Saddle Again." *Gone with the Wind* and *The Grapes of Wrath* were showing in theaters across the country, and a great debate was raging over whether to give England "all aid short of war" or to build a "Fortress America" in which to withdraw for safety.

The biggest issue facing Americans, however, was the 1940 presidential election, which pitted a president running for an unprecedented third term against a man who had been a lifelong member of one major party but who was nominated by another. Never before had an incumbent president sought a third term, and never again would anyone do so, for in 1951 the Twenty-second Amendment, which prohibited a third term, was adopted. It is also pretty safe to say that never again would such an unorthodox candidate emerge in such an unorthodox fashion as did the Republican candidate of 1940.

Franklin D. Roosevelt, the Democratic candidate, had seemed from his earliest beginnings to be destined for the presidency. His first brush with the office came at age seven when he was taken by his father, a staunch Democrat, to the White House to visit Grover Cleveland. "My little man," said Cleveland, patting Roosevelt on the head, "I am making a strange wish for you. It is that you may never be President of the United States." Much later, when Roosevelt won his first election (to the New York State Senate in 1910), the Tammany boss, Big Tim Sullivan, an enemy of Theodore Roosevelt, said of Franklin, "You know these Roosevelts. This fellow is still young. Wouldn't it be safer to drown him before he grows up?"

Franklin D. Roosevelt was first elected president in 1932 when Herbert Hoover was undone by what a J. P. Morgan associate called "a little distress selling on the Stock Exchange." Stocks lost twenty-five percent of their value in two days, one-third of the labor force subsequently became unemployed, and prohibition became a national joke. Roosevelt's New Deal was ushered in, despite Hoover's warning that with such an event, "the grass will grow in the streets of a hundred cities, a thousand towns; the weeds will overrun the fields . . . churches and schoolhouses will decay."

The third-term controversy raged for most of 1940. No president had ever been elected to a third term. A few had

FDR with his tilted cigarette, a pose that infuriated his enemies
(WIDE WORLD PHOTOS).

tried for it, as was noted in the anti-Roosevelt (Theodore, that is) jingle of 1912:

> *Washington wouldn't*
> *Grant couldn't*
> *Roosevelt shan't*

As the year wore on, Democratic presidential hopefuls, other than Roosevelt, and all the members of the Republican party grew more and more anxious about Roosevelt's intentions. He persisted in refusing to reveal them. The Republicans were especially interested since all the polls pointed to 1940 as their best year since 1928, but if "That Man in the White House" chose to run again, all bets were off.

The chief Republican contenders were Senator Robert A. Taft, son of the late president, and Governor Thomas E. Dewey of New York. Dewey was a rising young star of thirty-seven, of whom Roosevelt's Secretary of the Interior, Harold Ickes, remarked that he had thrown "his diaper into the ring." Another Republican candidate, the darkest horse in Republican history, was Wendell L. Willkie, a rank amateur in politics. He was also a Wall Street lawyer and the president of Commonwealth and Southern Corporation. But even more damning, only a year or so earlier he had been a registered Democrat, who in fact had contributed $150 to Roosevelt's 1936 campaign against Alf Landon.

The Republican convention opened in Philadelphia on June 1, two days after the fall of France and one day after the miraculous evacuation of Dunkirk. The platform was for "Americanism, preparedness and peace," and it condemned Roosevelt for his "explosive utterances," which were "leading us into war." The controversial aid-to-Britain plank promised "the extension to all peoples fighting for liberty, or whose liberty is threatened, of such aid as shall not be in violation of international law or inconsistent with the requirements of our own national defense." H.L. Mencken said of this plank that it was "so written that it will fit both the triumph of democracy and the collapse of democracy, and approve both sending arms to England or sending only flowers."

Next came the nominations. Taft was qualified as a loyal Republican, who according to his wife had "brains, character, and experience." Dewey, as a white Anglo-Saxon Protestant governor of New York, was an excellent candidate regardless of his age or any diaper remarks from Ickes. As for Willkie, he was forty-eight, dynamic, with a sense of humor, and it was said that he wore long underwear. On the other hand, no less a dignitary than Harvey Firestone had told him years before that he would never amount to a great deal because "No Democrat can ever amount to much."

One of Willkie's managers had fretted for almost a year over how he could make Willkie look good to the delegates: "They'll ask me 'Willkie, who's Willkie?' And I'll tell them he's the President of the Commonwealth and Southern. The next question will be, 'Where does that railroad go to?' And I will explain that it isn't a railroad, it's a public utility holding company. Then they'll say . . . 'now we know you are just plain crazy.' And that would be without my even getting to mention that he's a Democrat."

All of the candidates campaigned actively before the balloting began—especially Willkie, who defied tradition by actually attending the convention. One of the delegates he buttonholed was Senator Jim Watson of Willkie's home state of Indiana. "I admit I used to be a Democrat," Willkie said. "Used to be," snapped Watson. "You're a good Methodist," replied Willkie. "Don't you believe in conversion?" "Yes, Wendell," answered Watson. "It's all right if the town whore joins the church, but I wouldn't ask her to lead the choir the first night."

"We want Willkie! We want Willkie!" chanted his supporters. When the chairman tried to quiet them with the reminder that they were guests of the convention, they yelled back "Guests hell! We *are* the convention!" Willkie's amateurs did everything right, even to the point of having a really spontaneous "spontaneous" demonstration. When Willkie was nominated, at first nothing happened on the floor. All the frenzy was going on in the galleries. Nobody had thought of plans for the demonstration. This was quickly remedied by a New York delegate who tore that state's standard from the Dewey men and began parading around the floor. He was quickly joined by a small army, and a really spontaneous demonstration took place for twenty minutes.

The voting began with Dewey in the lead on the first ballot. Taft was second and Willkie was a distant third. Dewey faded with each subsequent ballot, however, and both Taft and Willkie gained. By the fifth ballot Willkie was in the lead, followed closely by Taft, and all the others were out of the race. The sixth ballot provided Willkie with victory, and there was bedlam in the hall. Thus Dewey became "the first World War II casualty," as a wag said later, and the Republicans had themselves an "odd" candidate, who unlike Roosevelt, "calls wah, war, and fahmehs, farmers."

The Democratic convention opened in Chicago on July 15, five days after the Battle of Britain had begun. Vice President John Nance Garner and Postmaster General James A. Farley were two of the announced candidates, but everything depended on Roosevelt, who was still keeping his plans to himself. To his inquiring secretary, Missy LeHand, he said that "God would provide" a candidate. Miss LeHand replied that God had better get busy soon. The time was at hand.

Roosevelt started things off by sending word to the convention that he had "no wish to be a candidate again," and that "all of the delegates to this convention are free to vote for any candidate." This was followed by chants of "We want Roosevelt," "Florida wants Roosevelt," and—evidently by a Republican—of "Willkie wants Roosevelt." A picture of Roosevelt was shown, followed by a demonstration lasting fifty-three minutes.

Even though Roosevelt "did not want to run," an anti-Roosevelt delegate, to be safe, introduced a motion that "no man should be eligible for a third term of the Presidential office." Since there were no women under consideration and both Grant and Teddy Roosevelt were dead, the motion was interpreted as being aimed at Franklin D. Roosevelt, and accordingly it was overwhelmingly defeated by a voice vote.

An aid-to-Britain plank was adopted, which was similar to that of the Republicans, and a platform promise was made not to "send our army, naval or air forces to fight in foreign lands outside of the Americas, except in case of attack." The nominations were made followed by demonstrations for each of the candidates. Roosevelt's was the biggest and the longest, and it was done to the tune of "The Song of Franklin D. Roosevelt Jones." On the first ballot, Roosevelt received nearly all of the 1,100 votes. The other candidates withdrew and the nomination was made unanimous. Thus Roosevelt was "drafted" by the Democratic party and Willkie got his wish to meet the Champ.

The fight over the vice-presidential nomination was more spirited, to say the least. It was understood that Garner would not be renominated, and that was fine with Cactus Jack, who later publicly declared the office as not being worth "a bucket of warm spit." (At least, spit was the word that appeared in the newspapers.) Roosevelt made it known that he wanted Secretary of Agriculture Henry A. Wallace, a choice that was received with mixed emotions by the convention. "Henry's my second choice," said one delegate. "Who's your first choice?" asked another. "Any son of a bitch, red, white, black or yellow, that can get the nomina-

tion," was the answer. In the end the anti-Wallace minire-
bellion blew itself out, and Wallace was nominated. One
factor in his favor was a gracious speech to the convention by
the First Lady, Eleanor Roosevelt. A second undoubtedly
was Franklin D. Roosevelt's statement to an aide: "Well,
damn it to hell, they will go for Wallace or I won't run and
you can jolly well tell them so."

Willkie kicked off the campaign with an acceptance
speech in his hometown of Elwood, Indiana. Before 200,000
people he accepted the nomination of the Republicans and
then proceeded to shock their right wing by accepting also

Willkie opening his campaign in Elwood, Indiana
(WIDE WORLD PHOTOS).

the major objectives of the Roosevelt administration. He "gave the Democrats hell," however, for their methods, denouncing Roosevelt for his conduct of foreign affairs and for courting "a war for which this country is hopelessly unprepared and which it emphatically does not want." "The New Deal has failed," he also said. He advocated the "philosophy of production" to replace the "philosophy of spending."

Norman Thomas, who was still running as the Socialist candidate, described Willkie's speech as a "synthesis of *McGuffey's First Reader*, the genealogy of Indiana, the collected speeches of Tom Girdler [an antilabor steel executive] and the *New Republic*." He accused Willkie of first agreeing with Roosevelt's entire program and then warning that it was taking the country straight into hell.

Some Republicans accused Willkie of endorsing the New Deal. One remarked that "every time Willkie opens his mouth he puts Roosevelt's words in it." Ickes called Willkie the "rich man's Roosevelt" and said that he made his acceptance speech at Elwood to convey the image of an Indiana farm boy rather than the "barefoot boy of Wall Street." A Republican senator responded by calling Ickes a "Hitler in short pants." Willkie replied that his office was "on Pine Street, a full block away from Wall Street."

"A vote for Willkie is a vote for Wall Street," one Democrat asserted. No, said others, "A vote for Willkie is a vote for Hitler." Thus the Democrats, who had been running against Hoover for twelve years, now added Wall Street and Hitler to their target area. As for Willkie, he was content to say that "A vote for Roosevelt is a vote for dictatorship." "Our democratic system will not outlast another four years," he stated, if "the third-term candidate" were reelected.

The issue of the third term was Willkie's strongest weapon, and he wielded it unmercifully. "The third-term candidate" has committed a "dictatorial" act, or "the third-term candidate" has committed an "act of war," he would

"The Sphinx—1940 Model" (Leo Joseph Roche; Collection Franklin D. Roosevelt Library, Hyde Park, New York. Reproduced in the *Buffalo Courier-Express*).

say. When the Democrats accused him of falsifying Roosevelt's record, Willkie charged that the New Deal had still left nine-million men and women unemployed. "Mr. Third-Term Candidate," he said, "tell the American people if Wendell Willkie falsified that part of the record." Signs appeared at rallies saying, "No Third Term," and they were answered by Democratic signs of "Better a Third Termer than a Third Rater."

Willkie's oratory got out of control on several occasions, as when he said, "Roosevelt is the great appeaser. At Munich what was he doing? Was he standing up, fighting for Democracy? Oh, no. He was telephoning Hitler, Mussolini, and Chamberlain, urging them to sell Czechoslovakia down the river." Then Willkie switched to attacking Roosevelt as a warmonger. "If his promises to keep our boys out of foreign wars is no better than his promises to balance the budget, they're already on the transports." He later issued a statement that he had "misspoken himself" on the Munich statement, but he stood pat on the other one.

Sometimes Willkie's flubs were more funny than shocking. In Cicero, Illinois, he began a speech by saying, "Now that we are in Chicago." Someone in the crowd yelled that he was not in Chicago, but in Cicero, to which Willkie replied, "All right, then to hell with Chicago."

The supporters of both candidates fired away at the opposition. Mayor La Guardia of New York said that he preferred "Roosevelt with his known faults to Willkie with his unknown virtues." Replying in kind, a Republican said, "the President's only supporters are paupers, those that earn less than twelve-hundred dollars, and the Roosevelt family." Roosevelt replied with unrestrained glee that we should forget the Roosevelt family, "but these Americans whom this man calls 'paupers' " constitute half of the American people.

A Republican committeewoman wrote, "Heaven help a war, if it is going to be run by Winston Churchill and

"Mother, Wilfred Wrote a Bad Word!" (Reprinted with permission from *Esquire* Magazine).

Franklin Roosevelt." Signs appeared at rallies reading, "Willkie for President—of Commonwealth and Southern," and "We Don't Like Eleanor Either." Democrats used Lincoln's argument against changing horses in the middle of the stream, to which Willkie replied, "Well, for one thing, what are we doing in the middle of the stream?"

Hate groups were active, too. Some people said Willkie was pro-German, and others even called him a Nazi. "Once a German, always a German," said still another, referring to Willkie's ancestry. It was said that Willkie's sister "was married to a Nazi" and that Willkie himself was anti-Negro. Hitler's statement, "Negroes are apes," was quoted in a way that indicated that Willkie agreed with it.

As for Roosevelt, his "real name" was Franklin Rosenfield," and he was "President of the 'Jew'-nited States" and former "Governor of 'Jew' York." He was also a "member of the International Jewish Conspiracy"—but then so "was Willkie," who must have been the only Nazi in the organization.

Willkie was even denounced as the "Candidate of Booze." A temperance publication carried the headline: "Every Booze Joint in the U.S. May Be Headquarters for Willkie." The evidence cited was that Willkie's two brothers were officials of the Seagram Distillers Company and that the candidate himself "likes a Scotch highball or two when he knocks off from work."

Roosevelt's strategy during the campaign was to be "presidential" by remaining at his desk and attending to the lofty duties of his office. "The Battle of Britain could not be adjourned by Roosevelt," solemnly explained Ickes, "in order to ride the circuit with Willkie." Roosevelt did engage, however, in a number of "nonpolitical" trips in which he delivered "nonpolitical speeches." In a political speech, he explained to Missy LeHand, one talks about politics, but in a nonpolitical speech the subject is government. Harry Truman was to say eight years later that he was getting ready to give a nonpolitical speech that was nonpartisan, but "one which the Democrats [of the area] will like to hear."

As the campaign entered its last few weeks, however, Roosevelt scheduled five major political addresses. Some said he decided to campaign because the polls showed that Willkie had a good chance of winning; a few even showed him ahead. But most observers believed Roosevelt's statement, "I'm an old campaigner, and I like a good fight." Declaring that he was exercising his privilege of answering the "more fantastic misstatements" of the opposition, he lashed out at the Republicans with the old Roosevelt master style. He pointed out that it was not his administration but the Republicans in Congress who had tried to keep us unprepared and who had fought against aiding Britain. "Great Britain would never have received an ounce of help from us," he said, "if the decision had been left to Martin, Barton and Fish [three isolationist Republicans]." Over and over he cited examples of Republican "faults," blaming them on "Martin, Barton and Fish." Soon the audience got into the spirit of things and repeated gleefully with him the cadence, "Martin, Barton and Fish," with the appropriate sneer on the last syllable.

In another speech Roosevelt spoke the lines, "I have said this before, but I shall say it again and again and again: 'Your boys are not going to be sent into foreign wars.' " His speechwriter wanted to add the phrase "except in case of attack," but Roosevelt refused. "Of course we'll fight if we're attacked," he said. If somebody attacks us, then it isn't a foreign war, is it? Or do they want me to guarantee that our troops will be sent into battle only in the event of another Civil War?"

On the election day Roosevelt had 27-million votes to Willkie's 22 million and won by an electoral vote margin of 449 to 82. Some Republicans blamed the "reliefers," saying

"You can't beat Santa Claus." Others blamed Willkie for a "me-too" campaign. It is more probable that "Americans who were frightened of Roosevelt were more frightened of Hitler." None of these analyses, however, give credit to the enormous confidence the people had in Roosevelt. As one historian said, "When Roosevelt said, 'My friends,' every listener believed him."

Willkie had no reason to feel ashamed of the result. He had fought a hard, skillful campaign, and even in his losing effort he received more votes than any Republican in history. It was not, in fact, until 1952, when Dwight Eisenhower won, that a Republican candidate did better. Willkie clearly had given the Champ the hardest fight of his three presidential election victories.

Roosevelt ran for president four times, against four different opponents. Of the four, Willkie was the only one he obviously both liked and respected. "You know," he said, "Willkie would have made a good Democrat. Too bad we lost him."

GIVE 'EM HELL,
HARRY

Every election is unique, but in some respects every election is similar to every other. The 1948 election, however, truly can be called unparalleled in the history of the United States. It was, for one thing, the biggest upset that has ever occurred in American presidential politics. For another, the incumbent president was the underdog, a rare happening, and his overwhelming defeat was predicted from the beginning of the year right up to and indeed through the election night by virtually every poll, every newspaper and newsmagazine, and every radio commentator. But in the wee hours of the morning following the election, as the humorist Fred Allen put it, "The polls went to the dogs instead of the other way around."

In 1948 World War II had been over for three years and the country was enjoying one of its greatest periods of prosperity. There were 40-million automobiles on the nation's highways, long-playing records were new and everywhere,

Harry S. Truman with the actress Lauren Bacall
reclining on his piano (United Press International Photo).

penicillin had come into its own as a miracle drug, the
transistor was invented, *The Snake Pit* was one of the biggest
movies of the year, "Your Hit Parade" and Bert Parks's "Stop
the Music" were two of the top radio programs, Citation won
racing's triple crown, and young Marlon Brando starred in
the Broadway play *A Streetcar Named Desire*.

On the negative side, the Cold War was at its height.
NATO was conceived that year, and the Berlin Airlift was
ordered. Runaway inflation and the high cost of living were
the domestic political issues. The Democratic president,
Harry S. Truman, was blamed for the inflation, of course,
but the Republican-controlled Eightieth Congress was also
on the defensive. Price controls had been lifted largely
through its efforts, and the cost of living had jumped thirty
percent since 1946.

As the time for the national conventions drew near, the confident Republicans were having a field day. "To err is Truman," they cracked. "Had Enough? Vote Republican" was a popular slogan. The pollsters were certain of a Republican landslide no matter who Truman's opponent was. "The election must be held," one newspaper editorialized, "if for no other reason than to find out which national pollster comes the closest." From the beginning of the year until the election night no one thought that Harry S. Truman would win—no one, that is, except Harry S. Truman.

The Republican convention met in late June in Philadelphia to nominate "the next President." Millions of Americans listened to the proceedings on their radios, and more millions in the Northeast watched through the new miracle of television. The leading candidates, as in 1940 and 1944, were Senator Robert A. Taft, now known as Mr. Republican, and Thomas E. Dewey, who was still the white Anglo-Saxon Protestant governor of New York and thus still formidable. Another major candidate was Senator Arthur Vandenberg, who was the leader of the Republican bipartisan group in the Senate. Vandenberg had formerly been a staunch isolationist, but he was slowly converted to internationalism, a process Secretary of State Dean Acheson called Vandenberg's "long day's journey into our time."

At first General Dwight D. Eisenhower was sought out as a candidate, but he took himself out of the race because "being a general was not the proper training for the Presidency," an observation that didn't do General Douglas MacArthur's presidential hopes any good either. Some said that Ike's statement at a "private" dinner that inflation could be curbed if businessmen would "forego profits for a year" dampened his Republican hosts' enthusiasm for his candidacy. At any rate, the statement was "leaked" to the big-business circles and Ike was reported as "disgusted" with politics.

Clare Boothe Luce, a keynoter at the Republican convention, got things going with the observation that Truman was "a gone goose," whose "time is short and whose situation is hopeless. . . . Democratic Presidents are always troubadours of trouble, crooners of catastrophe; they cannot win elections except in the climate of crisis." They thus have "a vested interest in depression at home and war abroad." Later Truman, accustomed as a Democrat to running against Hoover, found it strange that Republicans would mention the word depression in an election year. "You don't talk about rope in the house of one who has been hanged," he said.

Truman's other enemies found harsher things to say. He was "a squeaky-voiced tinhorn," Roosevelt's "ignorant successor," and in a speech of Taft's, "friendly to Fascist groups" and "soft on Communism." Representative Charlie Halleck made a strange statement: "There are a lot of people who find Truman is the poorest President since George Washington." There are a lot of others who find Washington was not so bad! The labor leader John L. Lewis said of Truman, "His principles are elastic. He is careless with the truth. He is a malignant, scheming sort of individual."

Dewey was nominated on the third ballot, and Governor Earl Warren of California was chosen by acclamation for the second spot. Taft had trailed badly on every ballot, because, some said, of the efficiency of Dewey's machine. Others blamed the chronic belief among many Republicans that Taft was "too conservative to win." A typical Taft philosophy that fostered this attitude was his "Let 'em eat beans" solution to the inflation problem. With the prices of meat so high, Taft said, low-income people could· change their diets. They could eat less, or "Beans could be used [instead of meat] . . . to lower the costs of meals." "Low-income people" took to this as much as businessmen took to Ike's suggestion that they forego their profits.

In nominating Dewey the Republicans broke with a strong

"A Good Man is Hard to Find"—Harry S. Truman with Dewey reclining on his piano (©Estate of Ben Shahn, 1983).

party tradition. They had never before nominated a candidate who had previously lost, as Dewey had against Franklin D. Roosevelt in 1944. The theory was apparently, as Alice Roosevelt Longworth observed, that "you can't make a *soufflé* rise twice." Dewey won the nomination, according to the columnist Max Lerner, "not because he had principles or even appeal, but because he had a machine [that was]... ruthless and well-oiled." He and Earl Warren proceeded to put this smoothly running machine in gear for a high-level, dignified campaign that they were certain would carry them to victory in November.

Amid placards reading, "I'm just mild about Harry," an unhappy Democratic convention, or as the *Detroit Free Press* said, "a quarreling gang of politicians" met also in

Philadelphia, on July 12. Senator Alben Barkley noted in his keynote address that Dewey "proposes to clean the cobwebs from the government in Washington. I am not an expert on cobwebs, but if my memory does not betray me, when the Democratic Party took over the government of the United States sixteen years ago, even the spiders were so weak from starvation that they could not weave a cobweb in any department of the government in Washington."

Before the convention met, a number of futile efforts were made to draft first Eisenhower and then Supreme Court Justice Douglas for the Democratic nomination. On the first ballot, however, Truman was overwhelmingly nominated, no doubt along the lines of Teddy Roosevelt's theory about Charles Fairbanks's selection as his running mate in 1904. Said Teddy, "Who in the name of heaven else is there?"

Truman's vice-presidential candidate was Barkley, who was willing but said, "I don't want it [the nomination] passed around so long it's like a cold biscuit."

A fight developed over civil rights when young Mayor Hubert Humphrey of Minneapolis demanded that the Democrats take the party "out of the shadow of states' rights and into the sunlight of human rights." To Truman's surprise, the strong Humphrey plank was adopted, with the result that most of the southern Democrats walked out of the convention. The left wing of the party had already rallied around the third-party candidacy of Henry Wallace. Now the right wing split away, too, and formed a new party. "Dixiecrat" Strom Thurmond, who was to be the candidate of the southern wing, was told by a reporter that Truman was only endorsing Franklin Roosevelt's past platforms on civil rights. "I agree," Thurmond replied, "but Truman really means it."

Newsweek magazine noted that before Truman's acceptance speech, "Nothing short of a stroke of magic could infuse the remnants of the party with enthusiasm. But magic he had; in a speech bristling with marching words, Mr. Truman brought the convention to its highest peak of excitement." "Senator Barkley and I will win this election, and make these Republicans like it," said Truman to a standing ovation. To Barkley he said, "I'm going to fight hard. I'm going to give them hell!"

Everyone wrote Truman off as a loser. *Life* magazine showed a picture of Dewey with the caption, "The next President of the United States." The *Kiplinger News Letter* stated flatly that "Dewey will be in for eight years." The columnist Drew Pearson predicted that Dewey "will be a first-class President." Even Walter Lippmann, one of the most astute political observers of the time, believed that "The best the Democrats can hope for is to survive as an opposition."

Many observers could not hide their glee at Truman's plight. "He has a right to his light-headed opinions," said the *New York Daily Mirror*, "but he has no right to hold them and be President of the United States. The voters, according to all indications, will take care of the matter." "The Democratic plight has its comic quality," said the *New York Herald Tribune* but warned the Republicans "to hold their laughter. The Democratic Party may be weak, but it does not follow that Mr. Truman is equally feeble as a candidate." As late as October 29 the chorus was the same. On that date the *San Francisco Chronicle* said, "It is a Godsend to this country and to the world at large that Harry Truman will get his dismissal notice next Tuesday."

Truman had a definition of what a presidential candidate should be: "First, he should be an honorable man. Then he should be a man who can get elected. Finally, he should be a man who knows what to do after he is elected." He believed he was a presidential candidate. It is one of the oddities of that odd year that everyone else discounted him, in spite of

Wallace, Truman, and the "machine" Dewey kick off the campaign
(Walt Kelly, in the *New York Star*; courtesy of Mrs. Walt Kelly).

the fact that he was the same Truman who made the momentous decision to drop the atomic bomb, who saved Europe with the Marshall Plan and the Truman Doctrine, and who ordered the Berlin Airlift and created NATO.

A vintage Truman performance was the tongue-lashing he gave Soviet Foreign Minister Molotov when they were first introduced. "I have never been talked to in my life like this," said Molotov. "Carry out your agreements," replied Truman, "and you won't get talked to like this."

It was a strange election. Dewey campaigned like an incumbent against an upstart challenger. Truman seemed to be an out desperately trying to get in. Dewey worked the theme of unity and "moving shoulder to shoulder" toward some unspecified Utopia. The polls told him that he needed only "to keep from losing," and so he was content to leave his audiences with such pearls of wisdom as "America's future . . . is still ahead of us" and "The highest purpose to which we could dedicate ourselves is to rediscover the everlasting variety among us," delivered at the Al Smith Memorial Dinner.

Truman traveled 31,000 miles and made over 350 speeches. He began with his acceptance speech when he castigated the "do-nothing Republican Eightieth Congress," and he announced that on July 26 ("Turnip day in Missouri") he was calling a special session to see "if there is any reality behind that Republican platform." The "do-nothing Republican Eightieth Congress" was his main theme throughout the campaign, but he also "poured it on" the "Wall Street reactionaries," the "economic tapeworms," and the "gluttons of privilege," who "stuck a pitchfork in the farmer's back" and "crudely and wickedly cheated" the people. "The Republican party," Truman said, "has shown in the Congress . . . that the leopard does not change its spots. It is still the party of Harding-Coolidge boom and Hoover depression."

AT BASEMENT LEVEL

"Give 'em hell, Harry!" (D.R. Fitzpatrick
in the *St. Louis Post Dispatch*).

"Give 'em hell, Harry!" the crowds would yell approvingly. "Well," Truman would respond, "I never give anybody hell. I just tell the truth and they think it's hell."

"The President is blackguarding the Congress at every whistle stop in the country," Taft said, which prompted the democratic national committee to conduct a "poll." The mayors of the "thriving, patriotic, modern, civic-minded, attractive and prosperous American municipalities recently described by Senator Robert A. Taft (Rep. Ohio) as 'whistle stops' " were asked to wire the committee whether they agreed with Taft's description of their cities. A number of replies were received and duly published:

Characteristically Senator Taft is confused, this time on whistles. (Laramie, Wyoming)

Seattle is not a whistle stop, but everyone who sees her stops and whistles.

If Senator Taft referred to Pocatello as 'whistle stop' it is apparent that he has not visited progressing Pocatello since time of his father's 1908 campaign for President.

Senator Taft in very poor taste to refer to Gary as whistle stop.

The term hardly applies to the Los Angeles metropolitan area in which presently live one-thirty-fifth of all the people in the United States.

The polls continued to forecast a Dewey landslide. An exception was the Roper Poll, whose owner conceded the election to Dewey early in the campaign and announced that further polling was useless. The experts therefore were puzzled by the large, enthusiastic crowds Truman attracted. Truman couldn't be taken seriously, in their view, so jokes and ridicule were used in place of explanations. "The President, in this critical hour," editorialized the *Washington Evening Star*, "is making a spectacle of himself in a political junket that would reflect discreditably on a ward heeler." A newsman observed that "With Truman's staff, Robert E. Lee couldn't carry Virginia." "How long is Dewey going to tolerate Truman's interference with running the government?" another asked.

An interesting detour occurred in Dewey's high-road campaign in Beaucoup, Illinois, when without warning his train backed up into the crowd. Fortunately no one was hurt—unless it was Dewey with the remark: "That's the first lunatic I've had for an engineer. He probably should be shot at sunrise, but we'll let him off this time." Truman needled, "Dewey objects to having engineers back up. He doesn't mention that under that great engineer, Hoover, we backed up into the worst depression in history." The irrepressible Harold Ickes, who had earlier labeled Dewey "the candidate in sneakers," (thereby promoting him from the candidate in diapers in 1940) added that the engineer had been listening to too many Dewey speeches in which Dewey wanted to turn the clock back to the days of Harding, Coolidge, and Hoover. "He honestly thought that Dewey wanted the train to run backwards too." The engineer had the last word. On hearing of Dewey's remark he said, "That doesn't change my opinion of him. I didn't think much of him in the first place."

Truman's audiences were friendly as well as large. On one occasion a woman called up to Truman on the platform of his train. "You sound like you have a cold," she said. The crowd yelled its approval when Truman replied, "That's because I ride around in the wind with my mouth open." In September a newspaper publisher visiting Truman in the White House, asked, "By the way, Mr. President, what exactly made you decide to run?" Looking around the room, Truman grinned, "Where would I ever find another house like this?" Toward the end of the campaign Truman told his audiences that he had a feeling he was being followed (by Dewey). He said he consulted his physician and was told not to worry. "There's one place that fellow's not going to follow you and that's into the White House!"

Dewey continued to be "Presidential," restraining his

running mate from calling *someone* an S.O.B. (as Warren said he wanted to do). Meanwhile Truman pressed the attack. "We have the Republicans on the run," Truman said. "Of course, the Republicans don't admit that. They've got a poll that says they're going to win." These polls, he continued, were "like sleeping pills to lull the voters into sleeping on election day. You might call them sleeping polls." People should vote for him, he said, "to keep the country from going to the dogs."

Finally the campaign, or Halloween, as Dewey called Truman's part in it, was over, and the candidates rested to await the outcome. Truman had changed the slogan from "mild" to "wild" about Harry, but still nobody seriously expected him to win. The *New York Herald Tribune* said that "Dewey has waged the most effective campaign of his political career." Drew Pearson said, "As a technician I would say Governor Dewey has conducted one of the most astute and skillful campaigns in recent years." The final polls showed Dewey certain to win. The major ones, Gallup, Roper, and Crossley, gave Dewey a lead of from 5 percent to 15 percent, and so did most of the state-by-state polls. Dewey was said to be leading in Iowa by 54 percent to 41 percent and in Illinois by 54.4 percent to 43.6 percent. The predictions of the *Fort Lauderdale Daily News* were so accurate as to be carried out to two decimal places, with the astounding result of Dewey, 62.96 percent and Truman, 23.15 percent! Curiously the "feed bag" poll and the "popcorn" poll forecast a Truman victory, but these were "unscientific" polls in which livestock feed customers of an Omaha feed company and popcorn customers in movie theaters were allowed their choice of bags printed with donkeys or with elephants.

Surprisingly the first returns showed no signs of a Dewey landslide. Truman was in the lead. The commentator H.V. Kaltenborn assured the country that "these are returns from a few cities. When the returns come in from the country the result will show Dewey winning overwhelmingly." But as the night wore on, Truman's lead continued to hold. Jim Farley, on a national radio broadcast, reiterated what Kaltenborn had promised, saying Truman "cannot win, for when the reports come in from the country—the Dewey strongholds—his early lead will fold up." The *New York Daily News* in its early edition stated that Dewey was headed "for a popular vote margin and a possible electoral vote landslide."

At midnight Truman was still leading. At 5:00 A.M. Dewey said he was "still confident." But when daylight came, Harry Truman was the winner. At 11:14 A.M., after California and Ohio had gone to Truman, Dewey conceded. Truman had 303 electoral votes to Dewey's 89. Truman even carried Florida, and by a three-to-two margin, in spite of the prediction of the *Fort Lauderdale Daily News*.

In his own account of the election night's events Truman said, "At six o'clock I was defeated. At ten o'clock I was defeated. Twelve o'clock I was defeated. Four o'clock I had won the election. And the next morning . . . in St. Louis, I was handed this paper [the *Chicago Tribune*] which said, 'DEWEY DEFEATS TRUMAN!' Of course, he wishes he had, but he didn't and that's all there was to it."

What went wrong? On the election night one man told a reporter that political experts were like weathermen. "The weatherman predicted rain tonight," he said, "and the political experts picked Dewey. There's no rain, and it looks like it might not even be dewey."

Truman's folksy manner, aggressive style, and spunk undoubtedly were large factors in his victory. Seizing the Eightieth Congress as the telling issue was certainly the most effective single thing he did. The Republicans couldn't conceal their record, Truman said later. It was like what Joe Louis said of one of his more elusive ring opponents, Truman added: "He could run but he couldn't hide."

The Morning After (United Press International Photo).

As for Thomas E. Dewey, he was an honorable man and a good campaigner, who was lulled by the favorable polls into waging the wrong kind of campaign. As he said later, "The American people basically want a blood-and-thunder campaign."

Mr. Truman's place in history as one of our better presidents is secure. "He was right on all the big things, and wrong on all the little things," said his friend, Speaker of the House Sam Rayburn. As time passes, the big things loom larger and the little ones are being forgotten. Winston Churchill told Truman in 1952, "The last time you and I sat across a conference table was at Potsdam. I must confess, sir, I held you in very low regard. I loathed your taking the place of Franklin Roosevelt. I misjudged you badly. Since that time, you, more than any other man, saved Western civilization." Truman wrote his own epitaph when he said, "I did my damnedest, and that's all there was to it."

THE NEW FRONTIER

The election of 1960 was in many ways the most remarkable election in United States history. Americans chose the youngest man ever elected president, forty-three-year-old John F. Kennedy, to succeed the oldest man at that time ever to hold the office, Dwight D. Eisenhower. The two major candidates were both born in the twentieth century— the first time that had ever happened; a Roman Catholic was the winner—another first; and the defeated candidate, Richard M. Nixon, was vice-president with one of the most popular presidents ever, and still he lost.

In 1960 times were good. The fifty-star United States flag was unfurled for the first time. *Ben-Hur* had won as best picture of the year. Ted Williams went into retirement with a home run on his last time at bat; Clark Gable made his last film, *The Misfits*; and in the news, a United States U-2 reconnaissance plane was shot down while assumed to be spying deep inside Russia. The world was in the space age, the Russian *Sputnik* having been launched in 1957 and having been followed by the American *Explorer* a few months later in early 1958.

Not only was 1960 in the space age, it was also in the television age. In 1950 only four-million American families had television sets, but by 1960 this figure had increased to 44 million (eighty-eight percent of all American families). In one respect, at least, the 1960 election was the television election. The two major candidates appeared face to face in four nationally televised "Great Debates," each with an average audience in excess of 65 million.

Kennedy was almost a campaign manager's dream of the perfect candidate. He had style and grace, and he was witty (on purpose, like Lincoln), handsome, well educated, and an authentic war hero. His PT-109 torpedo boat was wrecked by a Japanese destroyer in World War II, and Kennedy, the commanding officer, had saved the engineer's life by swimming for five hours with the engineer's life-belt strap clenched between his teeth. There was one problem, though, as was dramatically illustrated early in the campaign by a conversation Bobby Kennedy, John's brother and campaign manager, had with a group of Kennedy supporters. After going over the plans for conducting one of the early primary fights, Bobby said, "Well, what are our problems?" A man jumped to his feet and shouted, "There's only one problem. He's a Catholic. That's our goddamned problem."

Nixon, on the other hand, had no religious problems, and he was well known, a vigorous campaigner, and the heir apparent of the popular Ike. But he also had a flaw. His vigorous campaigning was considered by many to be "below the belt," and it had earned for him the reputation of a hatchet man and a nickname, Tricky Dick, which stuck to haunt him.

Kennedy knew that his religion and the fact that he was relatively unknown outside his home state of Massachusetts required that he enter every primary to prove to the party leaders that he could win. He had to win them all, and this he methodically proceeded to do. The issues, other than his religion, were his youth and his family's wealth. To defend his age, he noted that he had more government experience than "all but a handful of American Presidents, and every President of the twentieth century—including Wilson, Roosevelt, and Truman," before their assuming the office. If age, not experience, was the standard, then a test excluding those under forty-four would have "kept Jefferson from writing the Declaration of Independence, Washington from commanding the Continental Army, Madison from fathering the Constitution . . . and Christopher Columbus from even discovering America."

As to his family wealth, Kennedy laughed it off. To charges of "buying elections," he said he had just received a telegram from his "generous Daddy" reading, "Dear Jack: Don't buy a single vote more than is necessary. I'll be damned if I'm going to pay for a landslide."

Kennedy also kidded about the religious issue, as when he said, "I think it well that we recall what happened to a great governor when he became a Presidential nominee. Despite his successful record as a governor, despite his plain-spoken voice, the campaign was a debacle." The listeners, assuming he was talking about Al Smith, would roar their approval when he ended with, "To top it off, he lost his own state. . . . You all know his name and his religion—Alfred M. Landon, Protestant."

All the members of the large Kennedy family pitched in to help in the primaries. In West Virginia Kennedy's opponent was Senator Hubert Humphrey. Because the state was predominantly Protestant and critical to Kennedy, the family was extremely active. "They're all over the state," lamented Humphrey, "and they look alike and sound alike. . . . People think they're listening to Jack . . . in three or four different places at the same time."

The opponents of Kennedy and Humphrey hoped that their contest would be "a good clean fight from which no survivors emerged," but Kennedy won an inconclusive victory in Wisconsin and a resounding one in West Virginia. After that Humphrey withdrew. Kennedy took the remaining primaries and was the clear Democratic leader as the time approached for the convention.

Nixon, on the other hand, had only one obstacle in the way of the Republican nomination, Governor Nelson Rockefeller of New York. Rocky was cheerful, confident, intelligent, radiant, and rich ("I've never found it a handicap," he once said, "to be a Rockefeller"). He felt responsible for the welfare of the country. "I hate the thought of Dick Nixon being President of the United States," he said to an associate. Rockefeller discovered, however, that the more he actively campaigned, the more Nixon was kept in the limelight, and the better Nixon's chances became. Accordingly Rockefeller announced his withdrawal, adding that his decision was "definite and final." It was "definite and final," that is, (according to a Rocky associate) until the convention. The direct-challenge method would not have worked anyway, the associate said, "except by driving a personal assault on Eisenhower."

The Democratic convention met in Los Angeles in the first week of July, with Kennedy the overwhelming favorite. Senate Majority Leader Lyndon B. Johnson was his principal opponent, with Adlai Stevenson a sentimental favorite of many of the delegates. Also opposed to Kennedy was Harry Truman, who was backing Senator Stuart Symington. Truman thought Kennedy was too young, but mainly he distrusted the conservative politics of Kennedy's father. "I'm not against the Pope," Truman said. "I'm against the Pop."

When Adlai's name was placed in nomination there was a lengthy and emotional demonstration for him. "Do not reject this man who has made us all proud to be Democrats," pleaded the speaker, Senator Eugene McCarthy, and roars of "We want Stevenson" went up from the galleries. The Kennedys were not concerned, however, because they had an accurate count of the votes. "Don't worry, Dad," John said to his father. "Stevenson has everything but delegates."

Kennedy was nominated on the first ballot, and the party closed ranks around him—a most unusual display for Democrats. Johnson sent him a message saying, "LBJ now means Let's Back Jack," and Truman said, "I'm from Missouri. He had to show me and he did."

Kennedy's next order of business was to choose his running mate, and he surprised everyone by selecting Johnson, which caused an uproar and a near revolt among Kennedy's liberal friends. "What'll I say to all my friends in Boston," one said, "when they ask me why you picked Lyndon Johnson?" Kennedy smiled and said, "Pretend you know something they don't know." John Kenneth Galbraith helped smooth the ruffled feathers of the liberals with the observation, "This is the kind of political expediency Franklin Roosevelt would never have used—except in the case of John Nance Garner."

There was still the question of whether Johnson, the proud Senate Majority Leader, would accept an office referred to by its first occupant, John Adams, as "the most insignificant office that ever the invention of man contrived or his imagination conceived." Johnson's fellow Texan Sam Rayburn thought that without Johnson on the ticket, Nixon, whom he despised, would win the election. "I don't want a man who calls me a traitor to be President of the United States," Rayburn said. Finally Johnson agreed to run. Many observers think Johnson's effective campaigning was the difference in Kennedy's subsequent victory. "The farther south he campaigned, the thicker his southern accent became," one said of Johnson.

In Kennedy's acceptance speech he coined the name of his

administration. "We are not here to curse the darkness," he said, "but to light the candle. . . . We stand today on the edge of a New Frontier—the frontier of the 1960s. . . . Now begins another long journey. . . . Give me your help, and your hand, and your voice."

The Republican convention met in Chicago in the latter part of July. Ike had seemed lukewarm to Nixon's candidacy, noting to an associate, "The fact is, of course, I've watched Dick a long time and he just hasn't grown. So I just haven't honestly been able to believe that he is Presidential timber." In January he announced that there were "half a dozen, or

"Seldom has a candidate had so much experience at not being responsible for decisions" (from *Straight Herblock*, Simon & Schuster, 1964).

AUG 25 1960

HERBLOCK'S EDITORIAL CARTOON

"Seldom Has A Candidate Had So Much Experience
At Not Being Responsible For Decisions"

ten, or maybe a dozen, fine, virile men in the Republican party that I would gladly support." Finally in mid-March he endorsed Nixon, and so by convention time Nixon's nomination was cut and dried.

On May 1 Nixon had leaked to the press that Rockefeller was his choice for vice-president, possibly to head off Rocky's presidential candidacy. Rocky publicly spurned the offer, however, as he did the honor of serving as keynote speaker. At the convention Nixon chose as his running mate the United Nations Ambassador Henry Cabot Lodge, and his campaign strategy began to unfold. Nixon had just returned from Russia, where he had engaged in a "kitchen debate" with—and had pointed his finger at—Premier Khrushchev. Lodge had given the Russians hell in the United Nations at every opportunity. The Nixon-Lodge ticket would offer the voters experience and the ability to stand up to the Russians. In addition they tried to live down the old Tricky Dick past with a new Nixon image and to pretend they had never heard of the Republican party.

Kennedy and Johnson had to return to Congress, which was still in session, after the Democratic convention was over. There they plugged for medicare and other planks in the Democratic platform, but without success. Their real purpose was to get the session adjourned so they could take to the hustings. In the meantime Nixon was touring the Old South, explaining that southerners were not deserting the Democratic party but that the Democrats had deserted the southerners. He received an enthusiastic welcome, especially in Atlanta, where his campaign was "the greatest thing . . . since the premiere of *Gone with the Wind.*"

The Democrats revived the old Nixon image with a glowering photograph of the vice-president with the caption: "Would you buy a used car from this man?" Kennedy said, "With all this talk about an old Nixon and a new Nixon, it should be remembered that there was no old Lincoln or a

Would You Buy a Used Car from this Man? (Author's collection).

new Lincoln, no old Wilson or new Wilson, no old F.D.R. or new F.D.R. I cannot believe that the American people in these difficult times will choose a man with this fuzzy image of his own political philosophy."

Nixon stressed that party labels were not important. "I believe," he said, "that when we select a President of the United States that our history tells us that the American people look not just to party labels. They look behind them." In contrast Kennedy stressed party differences. "No Democratic candidate," he said, "has ever run and said, 'Parties don't matter,' because we are proud of our record. We want to be identified with it. We want to follow it." It was understandable, he declared, that Nixon would not want to be associated with Republican "stand-pat" slogans and candidates like McKinley, Harding, Coolidge, Hoover, Landon and Dewey. "Where do they get those candidates?" he asked his audiences.

Surprisingly, Kennedy encountered little heckling about his wealth. At one stop he thought he was going to get it when a tough-looking laboring man asked him if he had ever done manual labor for wages. When Kennedy answered that he had not, the man replied, "Well, let me tell you something. You ain't missed a damned thing!"

Nixon campaigned on his experience and attacked Kennedy for "downgrading America." He said the Kennedy program "would raise the price of everything the housewife buys by twenty-five percent." The program was too expensive. "It's not Jack's money he wants to spend, it's yours. . . . He may have more dollars but you have more sense."

"We can do better. We've got to get this country moving again," was Kennedy's theme. As to experience, Nixon's meant nothing, he said. He quoted Oscar Wilde's remark that "experience is the name we give to our mistakes."

Nixon made the most of his "kitchen debate" with Khrushchev. Kennedy was "too naive and inexperienced to stand up to Khrushchev," he said and chided Kennedy that he "would encourage Khrushchev and his fellow dictators to believe that this nation, the leader of the free world, is weak of will, is indecisive, is unsure of and hesitant to use her vast power."

"It is not naive to call for increased strength," replied Kennedy. "It is naive to think that freedom can prevail without it." He added, "Nothing I am saying will give Mr. Khrushchev the slightest encouragement. He is encouraged enough. The most ominous sound that Mr. Khrushchev can hear . . . is not of a debate in the United States, but the sound of America on the move, ready to move again." To his aides Kennedy joked, "Do you realize the responsibility I carry? I'm the only person between Nixon and the White House."

The religious issue was always present, of course, but it had its lighthearted moments, as when a Texas couple, visiting friends, were told, "I know you're anti-Catholic. I guess that means you're for Nixon." "We're not *that* anti-Catholic," was the reply.

More seriously, the president of the Southern Baptist Convention said, "No matter what Kennedy might say, he cannot separate himself from his church if he is a true Catholic. . . . All we ask is that Roman Catholicism lift its bloody hand from the throats of those that want to worship in the church of their choice." He added that "My church has enough members to beat Kennedy in this area if they all vote like I tell them to." The Reverend Dr. Norman Vincent Peale charged that a Catholic president would be under "extreme pressure from the hierarchy of his Church" to align United States foreign policy with that of the Vatican. Reinhold Niebuhr and John Bennett of the Union Theological Seminary denounced Peale's statement, accusing him of having "loosed the floodgates of religious bigotry." Adlai Stevenson said he found "Paul appealing and Peale appalling."

Kennedy, deciding to meet the issue head on, accepted an invitation to meet with the Greater Houston Ministerial Association. "I believe in an America where the separation of Church and State is absolute—where no Catholic prelate would tell the President (should he be a Catholic) how to act, and no Protestant minister should tell his parishioners for whom to vote," he told the ministers. "I am not the Catholic candidate for President, I am the Democratic Party's candidate for President who happens also to be a Catholic. I do not speak for my church on public matters, and the church does not speak for me."

The Houston speech impressed everyone who watched it, and though, as Kennedy told the ministers, "I am sure I have made no converts to my church," his speech probably made converts to his candidacy. "He ate 'em blood raw," said Sam Rayburn.

In the middle of the campaign Nixon was hospitalized with a knee infection, and Kennedy decided to soft-pedal his campaign while Nixon was indisposed. He pointed out later at a news conference that he had promised not to "mention him, unless I could praise him, until he got out of the hospital—and I have not mentioned him."

When Nixon was out campaigning again, Kennedy was back on the attack. "Last Thursday night Mr. Nixon dismissed me as 'another Truman,' " Kennedy said. "I regard that as a great compliment, and I have no hesitation in returning the compliment. I consider him another Dewey."

The high point of the campaign was undoubtedly the "Great Debates." There were four of them, with the candidates face to face on a national television program. The first one, on September 26, was on domestic issues, and Kennedy

The Great Debates (United Press International Photo).

opened it with his theme that the country could do better. He claimed that the economy was faltering, the country was stagnating, and our international position was deteriorating. We had to "get the country moving again," he said.

Nixon was cautious in his reply. "Our disagreement is not about the goals of America but only about the means to reach those goals," he said. He contradicted a number of Kennedy's statements, but in general he agreed with more than he differed with.

The most devastating question put to Nixon in the first debate destroyed the myth of his superior maturity and experience. The questioner, Sander Vanocur, recited a question put to Eisenhower at an August news conference: "What major decisions of your administration has the vice-president participated in?" He asked Nixon how he could explain Ike's answer—"If you give me a week I might think of one. I don't know." Nixon's answer was that if you knew Ike "that was probably a facetious remark," but the question itself had already done the damage.

Kennedy was calm, confident, and ready with informed, forceful answers. Nixon was equally well prepared, but he was on the defensive and seemed less assured. On one occasion, intending to say farm surplus, he said, "we must get rid of the farmer" and quickly corrected himself. The way he looked, however, was far more devastating than anything he said. Some said his face was made up—and it *was* in the succeeding debates—but for the first debate he had used only Lazy Shave powder to cover his five o'clock shadow. At any rate, he appeared "tense, almost frightened, at turns glowering and, occasionally, haggard-looking to the point of sickness," according to one writer.

In the third debate the question of Truman's profane language in the campaign was raised. Kennedy, to whom the question was directed, shrugged it off as a joke, saying that Mrs. Truman could get Truman to change, "but I know I can't." Nixon, however, had a detailed response: "One thing I have noted as I have traveled around the country are [sic] the tremendous number of children who come out to see the Presidential candidates... mothers holding their babies up.... It makes you realize that whoever is president is going to be a man that all the children of America will either look up to or look down to.... And I only hope that, should I win this election... whenever any mother or father talks to his child, he can look at the man in the White House [with respect]." It is ironic that Mr. Nixon, who was so concerned about clean language in 1960, was recorded on the Watergate tapes released in 1973 and 1974 in conversations containing one vulgarity after another. In the published transcripts of the tapes the vulgarities were replaced by "expletive deleted," a phrase that appeared so often it became a national joke.

As the campaign progressed, particularly after the first debate, Kennedy became more confident and kidded with the crowds. In one talk, speaking hurriedly, he repeated the same phrase three times in one sentence, to the amusement of the crowd. Kennedy also laughed and said, "We are going to put this speech to music and make a fortune out of it." Speaking to a group of Iowa farmers he expressed concern for their economic problems by asking in his Cape Cod accent, "What's wrong with the American fah-mah today?" As he paused for effect, someone in the audience answered, "He's stah-ving!" His listeners roared with laughter and so did Kennedy.

At the Al Smith Memorial Dinner, which Nixon also attended, Kennedy was in high form. He expressed pleasure that the dinner "could bring together amicably, at the same banquet table, for the first time in this campaign, two political leaders who are increasingly apprehensive about the November election—who have long eyed each other suspi-

ciously and who have disagreed so strongly, both publicly
and privately—Vice President Nixon and Governor Rockefeller." He continued with the observation that "the worst
news for the Republicans this week was that Casey Stengel
has been fired. It must show that experience does not
count." Stengel had managed the New York Yankees, with
ten pennants in twelve years—including 1960.
Kennedy concluded with a remark about Truman's use of
profanity in the campaign. "I have sent him the following
note: 'Dear Mr. President: I have noted with interest your
suggestion as to where those who vote for my opponent
should go. While I understand and sympathize with your
deep motivation, I think it is important that our side try to
refrain from raising the religious issue.' "

Toward the end Nixon, sensing that he was in trouble,
reverted to harsher language. "In the last seven days," remarked Kennedy, "he has called me an ignoramus, a liar, a
Pied Piper and all the rest. I just confine myself to calling
him a Republican . . . and he says that is really getting low."
Nixon also accused Kennedy of telling "a barefaced lie"
about the Republican stand on Social Security. To this Kennedy replied, "Having seen him four times close up . . . and
made up, I would not accuse Mr. Nixon of being barefaced,
but the American people can determine who is telling the
truth."

The polls showed Kennedy in the lead after the debates,
but in the last week Eisenhower joined Nixon's campaign.
Curiously, he had not been asked to do so earlier. "All we
want out of Ike," said one Nixonite, "is for him to handle
Khrushchev at the U.N. and not let things blow up there.
That's *all*!" Ike's last-minute appeals were, in Nixon's words,
"the most hard-hitting political speeches" the President ever
made. The last poll showed the candidates in a virtual tie,
prompting the comedian Mort Sahl to quip, "Neither candidate is going to win."

Although Ike's intervention hurt, Kennedy had little choice but to kid about it. Why did Nixon need Ike, Lodge, and Rockefeller, Kennedy wondered to his audiences, "to escort him through New York?" Why did he "not add Dewey, Hoover, and Landon?" or get Barry Goldwater "out of that Confederate uniform that he has been using in the South . . . and get him up North?"

On his own triumphal night in New York City, which attracted a crowd of 1,250,000, Kennedy called the Eisenhower-Nixon tour "Nixon Day in New York," and said it reminded him of "those elephants in the circus. They have their heads of ivory, thick skin, no vision, long memory, and when they move around the ring in the circus, they grab the tail of the elephant in front of them. Well, Dick grabbed that tail in 1952 and 1956, but in 1960 he is running, not the President. . . . I stand tonight where Woodrow Wilson stood, and Franklin Roosevelt stood, and Harry Truman stood. Dick Nixon stands where McKinley stood and Taft— listen to those candidates—Harding, Coolidge, Landon, Dewey. Where do they get them?"

In the last days of the campaign, Nixon promised, if elected, to go to Eastern Europe "to carry the message of freedom into the Communist world." When that idea failed to arouse interest, he proposed, on the day before the election, to send Eisenhower. Ike suggested that Hoover and Truman also go to make it a nonpartisan mission. Truman declined, saying such a thing "should have been done seven years ago." Kennedy's response was, "If I'm elected, I'm going to Washington, D.C., and get this country moving again."

Kennedy spent the last day before the election in New England, and he confined himself to serious discussions. In Connecticut he said, "At the time of the American Revolution, Thomas Paine said the cause of America is the cause of all mankind. Now in 1960 the cause of all mankind is the cause of America." He closed his speech with a quotation "which Lincoln wrote in a campaign very much like this, one hundred years ago. . . . 'I know there is a God, and I know He hates injustice. I see the storm coming and I know His hand is in it. But if He has a place and a part for me, I believe that I am ready.' Now, a hundred years later . . . if He has a place and a part for me, I believe that *we* are ready."

Kennedy was elected, with 303 electoral votes to Nixon's 219, but the election was one of the closest in history. Kennedy's popular vote margin was only 112,881 out of over 68 million. A shift of 37,000 votes in Illinois and Texas would have changed the result. Nixon waited until morning to concede, hoping for "a similar but reverse situation" to that of Charles Evans Hughes in 1916. Hughes had retired on the election night, thinking he had defeated Woodrow Wilson. A reporter calling on Hughes the next day was told, "The President is sleeping." "Well," said the reporter, "when he wakes up, tell him he isn't President."

The Torch is Passed—Eisenhower and Kennedy at the inauguration (United Press International Photo).

Lincoln weeping for Kennedy (by permission of Bill Mauldin and Wil-Jo Associates, Inc.).

The inauguration address was memorable. "Let the word go forth from this time and place, to friend and foe alike," Kennedy proclaimed, "that the torch has been passed to a new generation of Americans—born in this century, tempered by war, disciplined by a hard and bitter peace, proud of our ancient heritage—and unwilling to witness or permit the slow undoing of those human rights to which this nation has always been committed." He continued, defining the tasks facing the country and noting that they "will not be finished in the first hundred days . . . nor in the first thousand days, nor in the life of this administration, nor perhaps in our lifetime on this planet. But let us begin."

But a thousand days was all John Kennedy had before the senseless, evil act that took his life on November 22, 1963. His presidency was brief, and his critics say that it was "more style than substance." To his admirers, however, Kennedy's tenure is like the legendary Camelot described in the lines of his favorite song about King Arthur and his followers. Shortly after he died his wife, Jacqueline, made an observation with which most of John F. Kennedy's admirers would agree. She said, "There'll be great Presidents again, but there'll never be another Camelot."

☆ ☆ 13 ☆ ☆

WATERGATE

The story of the era between 1960 and 1980 in many respects is the saga of Richard Nixon—one of the most interesting in American presidential politics. From 1952 to 1974 Nixon figured prominently in every national election, running for president three times, for vice-president twice, and appearing as a top Republican spokesman in the off-year elections. His Watergate scandal, probably the worst in the history of the presidency, made Gerald Ford president, and by making the voters suspicious of establishment politicians, made possible the emergence of a rank outsider, Jimmy Carter, as the successful challenger in 1976.

Throughout the period the venom and the bilge continued to flow unabatedly. Barry Goldwater, the 1964 Republican candidate buried by the Lyndon Johnson landslide, was greatly impressed with the job the Democratic public relations people did on him. "If I hadn't known Barry Goldwater personally," he said, "I would have voted against the son-of-a-bitch myself." Johnson harbored no such bitterness—at first. "I seldom think of politics more than eighteen hours a day," he said in his happier times. But as the Vietnam War continued to drag on, with its damage to his popularity, he began to share Goldwater's feelings. "Cast your bread upon the waters," he advised a reporter, "and the sharks will get it." Despairing of trying to satisfy his many critics, he said, "I feel like a hound bitch in the country. If you run, they chew your tail off; if you stand still, they slip it to you." He ultimately confounded his tormentors by refusing to run for reelection.

Hubert Humphrey's 1968 candidacy was destroyed before it began by the abuse he took from the antiwar demonstrators and by the violence they suffered from the police at the Democratic convention in Chicago. He was even vilified by the Democratic liberals, his own brethren in the party. Many of them helped Nixon, his Republican opponent, by spending the campaign contemplating their own virtues, as one writer put it. "Choose if you can," said the *New Republic*, one of the nation's leading liberal magazines, professing to see no difference between Humphrey, the stalwart liberal champion for twenty years, and Nixon, his antithesis, who had built his career on the demogogic myth that Communists were taking over the government, and had more than once implied that Harry Truman was a traitor. The situation seemed so hopeless that a Humphrey aide, referring to the dissidents, said, "Nothing would bring the real peaceniks back to our side unless Hubert urinated on a portrait of Lyndon Johnson in Times Square before television—and then they'd say to him, 'Why didn't you do it before?' " Humphrey said after the election, "I could have beaten the Republicans any time, but it's difficult to take on the Republicans and fight a guerilla war in your own party at the same time." In spite of his horrible start, he almost won the election, losing to Nixon by less than half a percentage point.

Indeed the behavior of the liberals from 1960 to 1980 was

The 1980 choices (reprinted with permission from the *Minneapolis Star and Tribune*).

almost as remarkable as the career of Richard Nixon. In 1976 the Democratic liberal Eugene McCarthy almost undid the Democratic candidate, Jimmy Carter, by running as an independent and throwing four or five states to the Republican Jerry Ford. He would have thrown New York, and thus the election, to Ford if the New York Democrats had not succeeded in keeping him off the ballot. The liberals repeated their act in 1980, helping their archenemy, Ronald Reagan, defeat the incumbent Carter by rallying around the make-believe candidacy of Representative John Anderson. Early in the campaign New York's Liberal party guaranteed Reagan a chance in their state by giving Anderson their party's line on the ballot, the only time they had ever failed to endorse the Demoratic presidential candidate. "Anderson can win," stated the *New Republic* toward the end of the race, when everyone else thought—rightly, as it turned out—that he would not get a single electoral vote. McCarthy was still around, too. In one of the oddities of that odd campaign he actually endorsed Reagan! Democratic candidates after John Kennedy could not be faulted for concluding that the liberals were poor allies. The liberals had worked hard when the cause was hopeless, as for George McGovern in 1972, and when victory was certain, as for Johnson in 1964. But when there was a real race, such as Humphrey's in 1968 and Carter's in 1976 and 1980, they actually seemed to help the other side. Apparently, to paraphrase Franklin Roosevelt, the liberal motto of the period seemed to be: The only thing we have to fear is victory itself.

Gerald Ford, some said, was Nixon's revenge on the American people. At the height of the Watergate controversy, which ultimately did Nixon in, Vice President Spiro Agnew was charged with being a "common thief," as one of the prosecutors put it, and he resigned under the pressure of otherwise going to jail. Nixon chose Ford to succeed Agnew, but sitting behind his desk in the Oval Office he was quoted as asking a prominent Republican, "Can you imagine Jerry Ford sitting in this chair?" Ford did have a reputation for not being the smartest person in Congress, thanks largely to the efforts of Lyndon Johnson, who had accused him of playing football at Michigan too many times without his helmet. A more devastating crack was Johnson's charge, euphemistically reworded by the press, that "Jerry Ford is too dumb to chew gum and walk at the same time."

In the 1976 election Ford seemed to give credence to the rumors about his intelligence by continually bumping his head when boarding the presidential helicopter, pronouncing words like judgment with an extra syllable in the middle, toasting President Anwar Sadat of Egypt and "the people of Israel," and telling the voters of New Hampshire that "All Americans in all forty-eight, I mean forty-nine, states can learn from your example." In the middle of the next passage he explained that he of course meant fifty states. His worst and most costly gaffe in the campaign was his observance, in a nationally televised debate with Carter, that "there is no Soviet domination of Eastern Europe, and there never will be under a Ford administration." To show that this was not a slip on his part, Ford repeated this statement to the press the next day. By then the White House press corps had dubbed him "President Turkey" and accused him of "trying to sew up the klutz vote." Actually Ford was a very amiable and honest president with a below-average flair for campaigning. On one occasion, after one of his speeches, he said to a reporter, "Not worth a damn, was it?"

Ford's biggest mistake, however, which undoubtedly cost him the election, was committed before the campaign. It was

The Ford-Carter Debates (*Syracuse Herald-Journal*/Tim Atseff).

the September 1974 beauty: "I, Gerald R. Ford, President of the United States, . . . have granted . . . a full, free and absolute pardon unto Richard Nixon for all offenses against the United States which he, Richard Nixon, has committed or may have committed or taken part in." The pardon at once made Ford vulnerable, and he almost lost his party's nomination to Reagan, who contested it vigorously. Ford, "the man who pardoned Nixon," as Reagan noted, also was presiding over "the diplomatic and military decline of the United States," and was covering up his incompetence by promising all things to all people. "If he comes here with the same list of goodies as he did in Florida," Reagan told a North Carolina crowd, "the band won't know whether to play 'Hail to the Chief' or 'Santa Claus is Coming to Town.' " Reagan, in turn, was denounced by Ford as a warmonger who had advocated sending American troops to Vietnam, Angola, Rhodesia, Cuba, and Panama. "Governor Ronald Reagan couldn't start a war," a Ford ad said, but "President Ronald Reagan could." Carter contributed his opinion that it was "an almost unbelievable spectacle," with the "President of the United States deeply concerned about an ex-movie actor, traveling all over the nation to get a handful of delegates." He probably found it more believable four years later when the same ex-movie actor ran against him—and this time succeeded.

Ford's vice-president, Nelson Rockefeller, also made the news. He had bowed out as a candidate for reelection as a sop to the conservatives, but some of the more ardent ones wanted a categorical statement that he wasn't interested in the presidency even if something happened to Ford. "What would I do? . . . Resign? . . . that is the whole point of having a vice-president," replied Rocky. Later in Houston, at a private meeting of southern Republican state chairmen, he said, "You got me out, you sons of bitches, now get off your asses." Still later he capped his career in a way that must be

Rocky's farewell salute (United Press International Photo).

the envy of most politicians, by giving a group of hecklers the finger, recorded by the cameras for posterity.

Meanwhile Carter was running as a "peanut-farmer Billy Graham," who wanted "a government that is as good, and honest, and decent, and truthful, and fair, and competent, and idealistic, and compassionate, and as filled with love as are the American people." His workers asked, "Why Not the Best?" while Carter himself was content to point out that while he would not talk about Ford's pardoning of Nixon—

Ford had—there was "almost complete continuity" in policy in the "Nixon-Ford administration." Was it fair to link Ford to a man who was "fairly unsavory?" asked a reporter, to whom Carter replied, "It's not my fault that Nixon is unsavory."

Not to be outdone by Ford's gaffes, Carter began a series of his own. The most notable, and the one that played the largest role in dissipating his huge lead in the polls, was his incredible interview with *Playboy* magazine. "I've looked on a lot of women with lust. I've committed adultery in my heart many times," the Democratic candidate said, "and God forgives me for it." But he couldn't condemn a man who "leaves his wife and shacks up with somebody out of wedlock. Christ says, Don't consider yourself better than someone else because one guy screws a whole bunch of women while the other guy is loyal to his wife." The interview understandably caused an uproar, particularly among Carter's evangelical friends. Carter's own pastor lamented his choice of words, and a New York minister, evidently inexperienced with sexual slang, thought it *was* acceptable to condemn a man for "shacking down" with another man's wife.

Carter managed to hang on and win the election, but by an even smaller electoral margin than John Kennedy's in 1960. He enjoyed the usual "honeymoon" with Congress and the voters, beginning with his historic walk down Pennsylvania Avenue after the inauguration. But by 1980 the twin devils of inflation and energy had taken their toll on his presidency. He became the first incumbent to be seriously challenged for his party's renomination since William Howard Taft in 1912, and the first elected incumbent since Herbert Hoover to be denied reelection by the voters. He was blamed for all the country's ills, and the prevailing sentiment seemed to be as bad as that expressed by a writer who in 1892 called then President Benjamin Harrison "a purely intellectual being" with "no bowels," whose reelection would mean "four more years in a dripping cave." (People must not have liked Harrison's successor, Grover Cleveland, much more, for on the day his term ended, one said, "On this auspicious day the sky is blue, the birds sing and joy is unconfined. It is the last day of the Cleveland administration.")

In 1980 there were for the first time fifty-one primaries and caucuses, and thus it could be said that the voters chose the candidates as well as the winner. The exception perhaps was Anderson, the third candidate, who seemed to have been chosen by Reagan. At any rate, Anderson helped Reagan by splitting the moderate vote in the Republican primaries and by providing the Democratic liberals with a place to safely deposit their votes in the general election.

Although the voters had picked the candidates, they quickly repented and adopted a "plague on both your houses" attitude toward Carter and Reagan. "May the worst

Reagan's and Carter's views of each other
(*Syracuse Herald-Journal*/Tim Atseff).

man lose" seemed to be the popular view, and the slogan of
Richard Tuck, a political prankster, was "Nixon in '80—Why
not the worst?" The campaign was so dull that *Newsweek* ran
an article that tried to interest its readers in "the joy of non
sex," a prospect that seemed as exciting as the choices for
president.

There was indeed very little humor in the campaign.
Reagan got off one recorded joke when he pointed out that
the third-century Roman emperor Diocletian had tried price
controls and that they hadn't worked then either. "And I'm
the only one here old enough to remember that," he added.
His other jokes were unintentional, as when he indicted the

The public's view of the candidates
(*Syracuse Herald-Journal*/Tim Atseff).

redwood trees for producing more pollution than the auto-mobile manufacturers and when he cited the requirement of driver's licenses as evidence of our loss of freedom under the Democrats. He probably refrained from cracking jokes, and wisely so, because he didn't want to add to his reputation as a glib actor whose candidacy itself was a joke. Carter, on the other hand, was as evangelical as he was in 1976. His situation—being almost out of the race from the beginning, according to the polls—was certainly no laughing matter. He did provide one chuckle, however, in his acceptance speech, when he referred to Hubert Humphrey as that great American senator, "Hubert Horatio Hornblower."

Part of Carter's grim task was to keep the public from knowing of Anderson's candidacy, a job made more difficult daily as the newscasters kept referring to Carter, Reagan, and Anderson as the "three major candidates." The League of Women Voters added their bit to Carter's Anderson problem by inviting the "three major candidates" to engage in a debate. The League, whom in his earlier days Reagan had referred to as a bunch of "Rhine Maidens," issued their invitation just after the Democratic convention ended, at a time when the momentum was clearly with Carter and he had seemed to close the awesome gap in the polls. There was no way for Carter to run an intelligent campaign and at the same time accept such a suicidal offer to debate, and thus he refused. The "debate" was held anyway between Reagan and Anderson, and Carter's bandwagon never got back on track.

The final irony of the campaign came in the last week, when Carter did agree to debate. Apparently the lesson will never be learned that an incumbent president looms larger in the voters' eyes than his challenger until they appear together in debate. Though Carter looked "Presidential" and highly knowledgeable, the result was a disaster for him. The contest went from a horse race to a Reagan electoral landslide. Carter, an honest and highly intelligent man, had worked hard to be a good president, but the times were difficult, and the voters yearned for a change. They seemed, however, reluctant to vote for Reagan because he was perceived as a trigger-happy extremist. This perception changed during the debate when he came across as an amiable, reasonable candidate, and the voters then saw no reason to continue withholding their support from him. (Reagan's good showing might also be attributed to the fact, which came out in 1983, that his side had unethically obtained—not to say stolen—a copy of Carter's briefing notebook for the debate.)

The 1960 to 1980 era, as has been noted, was dominated by Richard Nixon. He had a checkered career, careening from one crisis to another like a person stricken with the disease of alcoholism, and charging his opponents with smearing him and being charged by them with lying, deceitfulness, and trickery. It all began in 1946 with an appearance before a California group in response to their newspaper ad seeking a candidate to run for Congress. He spoke of the American system of "government control" of our lives "advocated by the New Deal" as opposed to the one which "calls for individual freedoms and all that initiative can produce." Concluding, he said, "I hold with the latter viewpoint. I believe the returning veterans—and I have talked to many of them in the foxholes—will not be satisfied with a dole or a government handout."

Nixon served in the Navy, in the rear echelons of the Pacific, and could never have seen a foxhole in the first place. In the second place, would a man in a foxhole be entertaining guests? Would he be discussing economic philosophies? The group endorsed Nixon, nevertheless, and thus his career was launched.

The late forties and early fifties was a sordid era in American politics, when many second-rate men gained and held power by running on the single issue that their opponents were Communists themselves or were unwittingly doing the Communists' work for them. Nixon and his campaign manager, Murray Chotiner, seem to have been the first to use these tactics exclusively, but their success quickly attracted others like George Smathers in Florida and, of course, Joe McCarthy in Wisconsin. Smathers, in an especially crude anti-Communist campaign against the incumbent Senator Claude Pepper, ran "on the principle of the free state against the jail state." Pepper, he said, "is now on trial in Florida. Arrayed against him will be loyal Americans." On Pepper's side would be "all the socialists, all the radicals, and all the fellow travelers." In at least one speech, to what he considered an unsophisticated audience, he used the truth: "Are you aware that Claude Pepper is known all over Washington as a shameless extrovert? Not only that, but this man is reliably reported to practice nepotism with his sister-in-law, and he has a sister who was once a thespian. . . . Worst of all, it is an established fact that Mr. Pepper, before his marriage, practiced celibacy."

Nixon and Chotiner, however, were four years ahead of Smathers. In their successful 1946 Congressional election against the incumbent Jerry Voorhis, they ran the country's first unabashed single-issue, anti-Communist campaign. In Nixon's words, Voorhis was "a lip-service American" fronting for "un-American elements, wittingly or otherwise," who was "consistently voting the Moscow-PAC-Henry Wallace line in Congress." It did not matter that Voorhis was a staunch anti-Communist whom the PAC (Political Action Committee) specifically *refused* to endorse—Nixon continued to pound on this theme throughout the race. There were actually two PACs in California, both left wing and both vehemently opposed to Voorhis, but nobody except poor Voorhis seemed interested in the facts. Voorhis "was endorsed by the PAC and allied with the left-wing group which had taken over the Democratic Party in California," proclaimed Nixon. "A vote for Nixon is a vote against the Communist-dominated PAC with its gigantic slush fund," claimed the Nixon ads. In the final days anonymous phone calls were made throughout the district in which the caller would ask, "Did you know Jerry Voorhis was a Communist?" Nixon's managers denied responsibility for the calls, but at least one caller claimed to have worked out of the Republican headquarters.

Nixon's successful 1950 Senate race against Helen Gahagan Douglas was even more vicious than the Voorhis campaign. Again there was only one issue for Nixon: Was his opponent a Red? Douglas was labeled the pink lady, and "pink sheets" were distributed by the thousands explaining her "Communist" connections. She had, it seems, "generally been found voting in the House of Representatives with Vito Marcantonio [the most extreme left-wing Congressman at the time]." She was not just voting with him but was "found voting" with him, a much more serious matter. For example, they both were "found voting" for a bill to provide milk for the lunches of schoolchildren. (Indeed, if anyone had looked, Nixon himself could have been found voting with Marcantonio over fifty percent of the time.) There was, in fact, according to Nixon, a "Douglas-Marcantonio axis" in the Congress, "voting time after time against measures that are for the security of this country." To cap the campaign, Nixon brought Joe McCarthy into California for one day to contribute his opinion that "The chips are down between the American people and the Administration Commicrat Party of betrayal."

Nixon won the election, but not without some cost to himself. In the heat of the campaign a small southern California newspaper, the *Independent Review*, gave him the label Tricky Dick Nixon, and it stuck. It was, as one writer said, "too appropriate to be ignored."

Nixon's next crisis in preparation for the Watergate period came in 1952 when he was running for vice-president on General Eisenhower's presidential ticket. The general was taking the high road in the campaign, and Nixon characteristically was mining the old Communists-in-government theme for whatever nuggets he could find, when early in the campaign it came to light that Nixon was the beneficiary of a secret fund. It was a fund set up by a number of rich contributors for Nixon's use "to do the kind of selling job we wanted," as one of them put it. Nixon, in typical Chotiner fashion, brushed aside the issue, but its impact hit the Eisenhower entourage with devastating force and left the general "staggered and shaken."

It became clear from the Eisenhower group's reaction that Nixon had to explain himself—be "clean as a hound's tooth"—or be dropped from the ticket. Explaining that the "smear" on his record was coming from the "Communists and crooks" in the Truman administration, Nixon scheduled a nationwide television speech, known thereafter as "the Checkers speech," to explain the secret fund. The gist of his defense was not to deny any of the charges—they all seemed to be true—but to explain that the fund was used to pay expenses that legally could not be charged to the government. This was an incredible defense, but it seemed to work. "Not one cent of that money went for my personal use," he said, but in fact every penny had gone to his personal use, as he proceeded to make clear in outlining what the uses were. Toward the end he used his little dog Checkers as another example of a gift to the Nixon family. "Regardless of what they say about it, we're gonna keep it," he said. The remainder of the speech was an attack on his accusers, and the result of all of it was that he was kept on the ticket. "You're my boy," Ike told him two days later, and the secret fund controversy was over.

"Here he comes now" (from *Herblock's Here and Now*, Simon and Schuster, 1955).

Nixon's career seemed to be over in 1962, after his 1960 loss to John Kennedy, when he lost his bid to obtain the California governorship. Some people thought he wanted the governorship as a base for a 1964 presidential candidacy, but more likely he meant it when he pledged to serve out a full term if he won. (His reputation by then was like that of the boy who cried wolf: Nobody believed him even when he was being truthful.) Kennedy looked unbeatable at the time, and it was good politics to have an excuse not to run until 1968. The incumbent governor, Pat Brown, looked extremely vulnerable in a race against an ex-vice-president who had just missed being president by a whisker.

One of the low points of the 1962 campaign was the use of a cropped photograph by Nixon and his campaign manager, H. R. (Bob) Haldeman, showing Brown genuflecting to a Laotian girl in an earlier charity drive for refugees. The photograph was made more effective for Nixon's purpose by substituting Soviet Premier Khrushchev for the Laotian girl. Haldeman defended their action when it was exposed by pointing out that it was, after all, a picture of Brown.

The lowest point was Nixon and Haldeman's attempt to trick Democrats into voting Republican by the use of a fraudulent postcard "poll." They organized a "Committee for the Preservation of the Democratic party in California" as an instrument for mailing 500,000 postcards to conservative California Democrats, soliciting their opinion of the "capture" of the Democratic party by left-wing elements. (In most of Nixon's campaigns there was a group of "Democrats for Nixon," or a Democrats-for-something-other-than-Democrats group. It has been suggested that if Nixon had helped the Nazis there would doubtless have been a group of "Jews for Hitler" in Germany in 1933.) The idea was to publicize the predictable results of the "poll" as the majority opinion of all California Democrats.

The cards began with "Dear Fellow Democrat," and it was made perfectly clear that "This is not a plea for any candidate." The "capture" of the Democratic party by "this left-wing minority" was then described, and the reader was asked, "as a Democrat, what do you feel we can do?" An innocent suggestion was added that "we can take acceptable Republicans—if we can find any." The only Republican in the governor's race was, of course, Nixon.

The scheme was discovered when a Nixon volunteer worker, assuming the cards she was addressing actually came from the Democrats, took them to the Democratic headquarters in San Francisco. A court order was obtained to stop further mailing of the postcards and to stop the proposed publication of the results. The Democrats accepted an out-of-court settlement after the election, but the presiding judge filed his final judgment, naming Nixon and Haldeman as having "approved the [postcard] plan and project" and agreeing that the Republicans "would finance the project." There is almost no doubt that the judge would have convicted Nixon and ended his career then and there had the case not been dropped.

Thanks in part to the aborting of the "postcard poll" project, Nixon was soundly defeated by Brown. He suddenly decided on the morning after the election to tell the press off for its years of malice toward him. "Now that all the members of the press are so delighted that I have lost, I'd like to make a statement of my own," he began, and he ended fifteen minutes later with, "You won't have Nixon to kick around anymore, because, gentlemen, this is my last press conference."

In one of the greatest miracles of American politics, Nixon rose from these ashes to become his party's nominee in the 1968 presidential election. This he was able to do because of the leadership vacuum left by the Goldwater debacle and in spite of such protests as "He hath lain four years in his grave, wherefore he stinketh." Nixon won the election, hiring admen to package him and advertise him the way they would any other marketable commodity. His managers' only problem throughout the campaign was Nixon himself, whom rejected "as a reflex." "He says such incredible pap," one adman said, that any hopes for success required "creating an image without saying anything." Nixon "will be elected on what he didn't say," the theme ran. "What he says is gobbledygook anyway, of course." Everything was carefully programmed and controlled, even to the "spontaneous" Nixon responses in his many television round-table discussions and his closing telethon. In the latter event, Nixon had a set of answers on cards and his staff had the questions already written out. When a viewer called in with a question similar to theirs, the staff read their own question and attributed it to the caller. Nixon, of course, was ready with the answer. "This is the way they'll be elected forevermore," one Nixon adman said, and he added with uncanny accuracy, "The next guys up will be performers."

For the most part the Nixon campaign was a smooth operation, but there were occasional disagreements among his managers, some of whom objected to the use of "every goddamned cliché in the book." But the prevailing view was that the dissenters were "asses" who "missed the whole point." The Nixon ads were "meant to be trite." They had to be for their intended audience: "persons like Spiro Agnew who had never made an original observation in their life. . . . John Wayne may sound bad to the people in New York, but he sounds great to the schmucks we're trying to reach . . . the people down there along the Yahoo Belt."

The most remarkable feature of Nixon's 1968 victory was undoubtedly his ability to conduct the campaign without taking a stand on the most burning issue of the day—the Vietnam War. He insisted from the beginning that he had a "secret plan" for ending the war but for security reasons he could not reveal it to the voters until they elected him. That he never had to reveal his plan—or discuss whether he ever had one—and still he won is a tribute to his managers' ability to isolate him from the press and the public while at the same time making it appear that his campaign was the most open in history.

The last crisis (as of this writing) in Nixon's career, the

Watergate scandal, was brought on in the 1972 campaign by the arrests of a number of Republican operatives caught in the process of bugging the Democratic party headquarters in the Watergate office-and-apartment complex. Attorney General John Mitchell was first blamed, perhaps, as one observer suggested, on the theory that he "was the only politician in Washington ignorant enough to think there was something worth listening to at the Democratic National Committee." After his record landslide victory, however, Nixon himself was soon engulfed by the scandal. A Senate committee was formed to investigate the Watergate charges and consider the questions constantly put before it by Republican Senator Howard Baker: "What did the president know and when did he know it?"

During the course of the investigation it was discovered that for three years Nixon secretly had taped all his conversations without any of his visitors' knowledge or consent. Thus the tapes could answer both of Senator Baker's questions, but in the name of national security Nixon felt it wise not to make them available. As the tapes were extracted a few at a time under court order it was discovered that many previous Nixon statements were "inoperative" (not true) or "at variance" with the facts (lies), and that eighteen-and-one-half minutes of one of the most crucial tapes—the one recording Nixon's first conversation with Haldeman after the Watergate break-in—had been manually erased five to nine times. A "sinister force" was responsible for the gap in the tape, according to Nixon's top White House assistant, General Alexander Haig, but only Nixon, Haldeman, and one other aide had access to the tapes.

To add to Nixon's problems, the Watergate investigation brought out a number of financial irregularities in his affairs. Questions were raised about government spending to improve his two homes and about the backdating of deeds involved in the donation of his vice-presidential papers to

(From *Herblock Special Report*, W.W. Norton & Co., Inc., 1974).

the National Archives. In the fall of 1973, in a series of public appearances ironically dubbed Operation Candor, Nixon responded to questions about his finances and made the remarkable statement, "I am not a crook," a point that no other president has ever felt the need to make. He later bragged about his handling of his job in the midst of Watergate, saying "the tougher it gets the cooler I get."

Providence was getting ready to supply him with plenty of opportunities to get cooler.

In mid-1974 a House committee voted a bill of impeachment of Nixon. But Baker's questions were still unanswered, and Nixon's supporters in the House demanded to see the "smoking gun" evidence of Nixon's guilt. The "smoking gun" was produced in the form of the June 23, 1972 tape with Haldeman's suggestion that Nixon tell the FBI "to stay the

"I have just discovered that according to a secret tape of June 23, 1972, I *am* a crook." (Bill Sanders, *Milwaukee Journal*).

hell out of this," to which Nixon replied, "All right, fine." Nixon's support in Congress immediately collapsed. His most loyal supporter, Congressman Wiggins, asked sarcastically, "Does he have another Checkers speech in him?" and Senator Baker's questions were answered: What did the president know? Everything. When did he know it? From the beginning.

Shortly after the "smoking gun" appeared, Richard Nixon ended his presidency, as no man has ever done, with a letter to the Secretary of State:

Dear Mr. Secretary: I hereby resign the Office of President of the United States. Sincerely, Richard Nixon.

Nixon's life thus far may be summed up as Winston Churchill summed up that of Stanley Baldwin, the frequent prime minister of England: "He occasionally stumbles over the truth but he always hastily picks himself up as if nothing had happened." Harry Truman put it more directly over twenty years before Watergate. "Nixon is a shifty-eyed, goddamn liar," he said, and to bring the voters up to date he noted during the 1960 campaign that anyone who voted for Nixon "ought to go to hell. . . . Nixon never told the truth in his life." John Sirica, the judge in the Watergate trials and a Republican who had voted three times for Nixon, closed the chapter on Watergate with a wish shared by many of his fellow Americans. He said, "I hope no political party will ever stoop so low as to embrace the likes of Richard Nixon again."

☆ ☆ 14 ☆ ☆

WHAT NOW?

What does the future hold for our presidency? Can our democratic system continue to fulfill Chester Congdon's hope of always having a president "that the dogs won't urinate on?" Considering the magnitude of the problems we face, these are not idle questions.

Since 1960 our system has been hit by a chain of almost incredible shocks, and we have witnessed unusual and unprecedented happenings. We have seen John Kennedy murdered in the streets of Dallas, Ronald Reagan shot down in the streets of Washington, D.C., Lyndon Johnson hounded from office by a war we didn't win, and Gerald Ford and Jimmy Carter unceremoniously kicked out by the voters. We have seen our first two unelected vice-presidents, Ford and Nelson Rockefeller, and our first president—Ford again—who was neither elected president nor vice-president. In the unusual category, we have elected, within a twelve-year period, two presidents, Johnson and Carter, from the deep South, and in 1980 we elected a sixty-nine-year-old ex-movie actor. Johnson and Carter were the first southern presidents since Zachary Taylor was elected in 1848, and Reagan, who turned seventy in his first month in office, was the oldest president ever to serve in our history.

In the disgraceful category we have had the spectacle of a vice-president resigning because of common-thief charges, and the unprecedented resignation of a president, under the threat of losing his $174,000 annual pension and benefits. We have heard a president lying, using barnyard language, and plotting crimes, recorded on tape in the Oval Office and played for the public. We have seen impeachment charges brought against a president for only the second time in our history, and in this case, unlike the first, the House would surely have voted for impeachment and the Senate for conviction had the president not chosen to resign. Finally we have seen one president pardoned by another, his hand-picked successor, not just for crimes he committed, but for any he *may have committed* during his presidency.

Besides Vietnam and Watergate, we have experienced the insulting 1973 Arab oil embargo and the more insulting 1980 seizure of our diplomatic personnel by the Iranian government. We have seen the steady erosion of our economic position to the point where a small country like Japan, with no natural resources, threatens our position as the number-one industrial power in the world. We have seen sustained double-digit inflation for the first time in our history that has the capacity to destroy our dollar, if not our economic system itself. Finally we have seen an energy crisis, which, as Carter said, is the moral equivalent of war, and which could ultimately threaten our nation's existence as it has not been threatened since the great schism that led to the Civil War.

An even more nagging concern is the fear that something

LINCOLN   FORD   EDSEL

Lincoln, Ford as himself (considered damning enough),
and Nixon as an Edsel (V. Roschkov, *Windsor Star*).

fundamental is wrong with our system and that our people
have lost confidence in our leaders and in our democratic
process. In 1980, despite the fact that the candidates were
chosen by delegates from fifty-one primaries and caucuses,
there was widespread dissatisfaction with the choices, and
fewer than half the eligible voters participated in the election. The crazy-quilt pattern of primaries contributed no
doubt to the voters' disillusionment, since the earliest ones,
with the help of the media, determined the candidates, and
the later ones, such as California's, which was the nation's
largest, were meaningless. Even more alarming are the signs
of political instability, as exemplified by our abnormal presidential turnover in recent years. From January, 1961 to
January, 1981 we had no fewer than seven presidents—
Eisenhower, Kennedy, Johnson, Nixon, Ford, Carter, and
Reagan—and no president since Eisenhower has served two
full terms in the White House. The last time we had such
instability was the period from 1841 to 1861 when no presi-

dent served two full terms and nine different men occupied the White House. This period, of course, ended with the Civil War. Is our situation, as the Englishman said, serious but not hopeless, or is it, as the Frenchman said, hopeless but not serious?

This is a good time to take heart. As bad as things may seem, the country has to be better off now than it was perceived to be in 1801 by Timothy Dwight, then president of Yale. Thomas Jefferson had been in office but a few months when the Reverend Mr. Dwight announced that "We have now reached the consummation of democratic blessedness. We have a country governed by blockheads and knaves; the ties of marriage with all its felicities are severed and destroyed; our wives and daughters are thrown into the stews; our children cast into the world from the breast and forgotten; filial piety is extinguished, and our surnames, the only mark of distinction among families, are abolished. Can the imagination paint anything more dreadful on this side of hell?" It is difficult to believe that it could.

In terms of material goods, we still have the most going for us of any country on earth. Ours is the richest and strongest country in the world. Our technology is second to none, as was shown by our placing men on the moon and the space shuttle in orbit—achievements no other country has been able to match. The farmlands of our Midwest are the best on earth, and we could probably single-handedly feed the entire world. We have oil and gas resources and with a small conservation effort, could be self-sufficient for a long time. We have more energy in coal than Saudi Arabia has in oil.

The future has seemed bleak before, and we've always had leaders who rose to the occasion. In December, 1776 General George Washington abandoned New York to the British and began his retreat across New Jersey with his ragtag army. Most of the American colonists probably thought their revolution was over before it had hardly begun. Thomas Paine, who was in Washington's army, wrote, "These are the times that try men's souls. The Summer soldier and the sunshine patriot will, in this crisis, shrink from the service of his country; but he that stands by it now, deserves the love and thanks of man and woman. Tyranny, like hell, is not easily conquered; yet we have this consolation with us, that the harder the conflict the more glorious the triumph." Johann Rall, the commander of the Hessians at Trenton, scoffed at reports that Washington's army was nearby, noting that he had nothing to fear from "these country clowns." But on Christmas night, in a violent storm, these "clowns" crossed the Delaware River and the next morning captured or killed the members of the entire Hessian regiment without the loss of a single American life. A brief review of the battle was issued by one of the Americans: "Hessian population of Trenton at 8 A.M., 1,408 men and 39 officers; Hessian population at 9 A.M.—0."

Our political woes of today cannot begin to match those of 1861, when states were seceding from the Union and a great war threatened to destroy our country. Again we were fortunate in our choice of leaders. After a string of mediocre presidents from Van Buren to Buchanan, with the single bright exception of Polk, Abraham Lincoln emerged, with the courage and determination to save the nation. "In your hands, my dissatisfied fellow countrymen, and not in mine, is the momentous issue of civil war," he said in his inauguration address. "You have no oath registered in heaven to destroy the government, while I shall have the most solemn one to 'preserve, protect, and defend' it."

Our economic troubles certainly have not reached the desperate depths of the Great Depression of the 1930s, when twenty-five percent of the working force was unemployed. At this point Franklin D. Roosevelt arrived on the scene and assured us that "This great Nation will endure as it has endured, will revive and will prosper. So first of all, let me assert my firm belief that the only thing we have to fear is fear itself." Roosevelt was at the helm on December 7, 1941, when the message was received that shook the United States as nothing had since the firing on Fort Sumter: "AIR RAID, PEARL HARBOR—THIS IS NO DRILL." We thus became the principal power in the greatest war the world has ever seen. Again Roosevelt reassured us: "Hostilities exist. There is no blinking at the fact that our people, our territory and our interests are in grave danger. With confidence in our armed forces—with the unbounding determination of our people—we will gain the inevitable triumph—so help us God."

To be sure, we have had some ordinary presidents, some below-average presidents, and three presidents—Grant, Harding, and Nixon—who were failures. But our system has also produced a disproportionately large number of great and near-great presidents, like Lincoln, Washington, Franklin D. Roosevelt, Jefferson, Jackson, Truman, Polk, Wilson, Theodore Roosevelt, and Kennedy. Most of our presidents have grown in office and been equal to the tasks demanded of them. They were there when we needed them. Perhaps Benjamin Harrison was right in his 1888 observation that "Providence has provided" for us. Thus the ancient quote used by John Kennedy in his last official words—his undelivered speech in Dallas—may be most appropriate: Unless the Lord keep the city, the watchman waketh but in vain.

We'll have great presidents again, as Jackie Kennedy observed in 1963, which is a good note on which to end. The Lord *has* kept our city, and "this great Nation will endure as it has endured, will revive and will prosper."

"They called me 'honest Abe.' What did they call you?"
(Ray Osrin, *Cleveland Plain Dealer*).

Despite a diversity of presidents our ship of state is still afloat.

As a final note on our presidents, we give in this section a picture of each of the thirty-nine men, from George Washington to Ronald Reagan, who have occupied our highest office. We also include for each president a short comment about him made by one of his contemporaries. We have listed the presidents in the order of their ranking according to a poll of forty-nine of the country's leading historians, conducted by writer Steve Neal, and published in the article, "Our best and worst presidents," in the magazine section of the *Chicago Tribune* on January 10, 1982. This poll lists the top ten and the bottom ten presidents as well as a general ranking of all the presidents. Since the two lists were obtained by different means, they are not entirely consistent; therefore we have used the top and bottom ten and filled in the intervening positions in accordance with the general ranking list. William Henry Harrison and James A. Garfield are unranked because of their brief tenure in office, and President Reagan is not ranked, of course, because he was the current president when the poll was taken. The ranking is as follows:

1. Lincoln	15. John Adams	29. Coolidge
2. Washington	16. Monroe	30. Andrew Johnson
3. Franklin Roosevelt	17. Madison	31. Fillmore
4. Theodore Roosevelt	18. Van Buren	32. Grant
5. Jefferson	19. John Quincy Adams	33. Pierce
6. Wilson	20. Taft	34. Buchanan
7. Jackson	21. Hoover	35. Nixon
8. Truman	22. Hayes	36. Harding
9. Eisenhower	23. Ford	Unranked:
10. Polk	24. Arthur	37. Garfield
11. McKinley	25. Benjamin Harrison	38. William Henry Harrison
12. Lyndon Johnson	26. Taylor	39. Reagan
13. Cleveland	27. Carter	
14. Kennedy	28. Tyler	

The photographs used are the official ones of the presidents, in most cases. Those of Eisenhower, Kennedy, Lyndon Johnson, Nixon, Ford, Carter, and Reagan are in the *Pocket Congressional Directory* issued during their years. Those of Washington, John Adams, Jefferson, Madison, and Monroe are copies of Gilbert Stuart paintings, and that of John Quincy Adams is a copy of a painting by Thomas Sully. The pictures of Taylor and Andrew Johnson are from engravings by Alexander H. Ritchie, and that of Buchanan is from an engraving by John C. Buttre. Jackson's, Van Buren's, and Polk's pictures are copies of daguerreotypes by Mathew Brady, and Lincoln's is a copy of a photograph by A. Gardner. The originals of Arthur and Wilson belong to the New York Historical Society; that of Franklin Roosevelt is in the Franklin D. Roosevelt Library. The remaining photographs are in the Library of Congress.

Abraham Lincoln 1861–1865
"A low-bred obscene clown." *(Atlanta Intelligencer)*

George Washington, 1789–1797
"The man who is the source of all the misfortunes
of our country." (The *Philadelphia Aurora*)

Franklin D. Roosevelt   1933–1945
He thinks the government is "a milk cow
with 125 million teats." (H.L. Mencken)

Theodore Roosevelt   1901–1909
"As sweet a gentleman as ever scuttled a ship or cut a
throat." (Henry Watterson)

Thomas Jefferson   1801–1809
"A contemptible hypocrite," with "pretensions
to character." (Alexander Hamilton)

Woodrow Wilson   1913–1921
"He talked like Jesus Christ, but acted like Lloyd George."
(French Premier Georges Clemenceau)

Andrew Jackson   1829–1837
"A barbarian and savage who can scarcely spell
his own name." (John Quincy Adams)

Harry S. Truman   1945–1953
"The poorest President since George Washington."
(Congressman Charlie Halleck)

Dwight D. Eisenhower   1953–1961
"He couldn't make a decision to save his soul in hell."
(Harry S. Truman)

James K. Polk   1845–1849
"A fourth or rather fortieth rate lawyer
and small politician . . . who by accident was
once Speaker of the House." (*New York Herald*)

William McKinley 1897–1901
"A white-livered cur with no more backbone
than a chocolate éclair." (Theodore Roosevelt)

Lyndon B. Johnson 1963–1969
He "had so much power and wanted so much more power
that Democrats didn't know whether to vote for him
or plug him in." (Barry Goldwater)

Grover Cleveland   1885–1889 and 1893–1897
"A coarse debauchee who would bring his harlots
with him to Washington and hire lodgings for them
convenient to the White House." (*New York Sun*)

John F. Kennedy   1961–1963
He impersonates "a prematurely elder statesman
who wants to grow up to be Lyndon Johnson."
(*New York Post*)

John Adams   1797–1801
"A semi-maniac . . . who in his soberest senses is
the greatest marplot in nature." (Theodore Sedgwick)

James Monroe   1817–1825
"A damned infernal old scoundrel."
(Secretary of the Treasury William H. Crawford)

James Madison   1809–1817
"A withered little applejohn." (Washington Irving)

Martin Van Buren   1837–1841
"A fop laced up in corsets, such as women in town wear,
and if possible, tighter than the best of them."
(Davy Crockett)

John Quincy Adams   1825–1829
"The Pimp of the Coalition."
(Andrew Jackson supporters)

William Howard Taft   1909–1913
"Fat son of a bitch, ain't he?" (Clarence Darrow)

Herbert Hoover   1929–1933
"In Hoover we trusted. Now we are busted."
(1932 placard)

Rutherford B. Hayes   1877–1881
"Rutherfraud." (Tilden supporters)

Gerald R. Ford 1974–1977
"The man who pardoned Nixon." (Ronald Reagan)

Chester A. Arthur 1881–1885
He "still stands at Albany under a sign which reads:
'Political dickering and other dirty work
done here!' " (John Hay)

Benjamin Harrison   1889–1893
"A purely intellectual being with no bowels,"
whose reelection would mean "four more years
in a dripping cave." (An 1892 contemporary)

Zachary Taylor   1849–1850
"Dead and in hell, and I am glad of it." (Brigham Young)

Jimmy Carter   1977–1981
He "couldn't get the Pledge of Allegiance
through Congress." (A veteran Congressman)

John Tyler   1841–1845
"His Accidency." (John Quincy Adams)

Calvin Coolidge   1923–1929
"The greatest man ever to come out of Plymouth Notch, Vermont." (Clarence Darrow)

Andrew Johnson   1865–1869
"Dirty as cart-wheel grease." (A radical Republican)

Millard Fillmore   1850–1853
"A vain and handsome mediocrity." (Thurlow Weed)

Ulysses S. Grant   1869–1877
His election gives us a chance to "see if there is
any difference between a drunken tailor [Andrew Johnson]
and a drunken tanner." (General Benjamin Butler)

Franklin Pierce 1853–1857
If he can be nominated, "no private citizen
is safe" from the office. (Stephen A. Douglas)

James Buchanan 1857–1861
"An able man, but is in small matters without judgment
and sometimes acts like an old maid." (James K. Polk)

Richard M. Nixon   1969–1974
He "should get his ass out of the White House—today!"
(Barry Goldwater)

Warren G. Harding   1921–1923
"Not a bad man. He was just a slob."
(Alice Roosevelt Longworth)

James A. Garfield   1881
"Not possessed of the backbone of an angle-worm."
(U.S. Grant)

William Henry Harrison   1841
Regret his death "only because he did not live long enough
to prove his incapacity for the office of President."
(William Cullen Bryant)

Ronald Reagan   1981–
"We'd rather have you say he's too ignorant than too old."
(John Sears, Reagan's campaign manager)

Abels, Jules. *Out of the Jaws of Victory*. New York: Henry Holt and Co., 1959.

_____. *The Degeneration of Our Presidential Election: A History and Analysis of an American Institution in Trouble*. New York: Macmillan and Co., 1968.

Acheson, Dean. *A Democrat Looks at His Party*. New York: Harper & Brothers, 1955.

_____. *Present at the Creation*. New York: W.W. Norton and Co., 1969.

Adler, Bill. *The Kennedy Wit*. New York: The Citadel Press, 1964.

Agar, Herbert. *The People's Choice, from Washington to Harding*. New York: Houghton Mifflin Co., 1933.

Anderson, Donald F. *William Howard Taft*. Ithaca, N.Y.: Cornell University Press, 1973.

Armbruster, Maxim Ethan. *The Presidents of the United States and Their Administrations from Washington to Reagan*. New York: Horizon Press, 1982.

Bailey, Thomas A. *Presidential Greatness: The Image and the Man from George Washington to the Present.* New York: Appleton-Century, 1966.

Bassett, Margaret Byrd. *Profiles and Portraits of American Presidents.* New York: McKay, 1976.

Bendiner, Robert. *White House Fever.* New York: Harcourt, Brace and Co., 1960.

Ben-Veniste, Richard and George Frampton, Jr. *Stonewall: The Real Story of the Watergate Prosecution.* New York: Simon and Schuster, 1977.

Boller, Paul F., Jr. *Presidential Anecdotes.* New York: Oxford University Press, 1981.

Burns, James MacGregor. *Roosevelt: The Lion and the Fox.* New York: Harcourt, Brace and Co., 1956.

Butterfield, Roger P. *The American Past: A History of the United States from Concord to Hiroshima, 1775–1945.* New York: Simon and Schuster, 1947.

Cirker, Hayward and Blanche Cirker. *Dictionary of American Portraits.* New York: Dover Publications, 1967.

Cohn, David L. *The Fabulous Democrats.* New York: G.P. Putnam's Sons, 1956.

Cunliffe, Marcus. *American Presidents and the Presidency* (2nd ed.). New York: McGraw-Hill Book Co., 1976.

DiSalle, Michael V. (with Lawrence G. Blochman). *Second Choice.* New York: Hawthorne Books, Inc., 1966.

Dorman, Michael. *The Second Man: The Changing Role of the Vice Presidency.* New York: Delacorte Press, 1968.

Duffy, Herbert S. *William Howard Taft.* New York: Minton, Balch and Co., 1930.

Durant, John and Alice Durant. *Pictorial History of American Presidents.* New York: A.S. Barnes and Co., 1955.

Eaton, Herbert. *Presidential Timber: A History of Nominating Conventions, 1868–1960.* New York: Free Press of Glencoe, 1964.

Ernst, Morris Leopold. *The People Know Best: The Ballots*

vs. the Polls. Washington, D.C.: Public Affairs Press, 1949.

Felknor, Bruce L. *Dirty Politics*. New York: W.W. Norton & Co., 1966.

Gable, John A. *The Bull Moose Years: Theodore Roosevelt and the Progressive Party*. Port Washington, N.Y.: Kennikat Press, 1978.

Gibson, Albert M. *A Political Crime: The History of the Great Fraud*. New York: W.S. Gottsberger, 1885.

Goodman, Mark (ed.). *Give 'Em Hell, Harry!* New York: Award Books, 1975.

Gunderson, Robert G. *The Log-Cabin Campaign*. Lexington: University of Kentucky Press, 1957.

Harwood, Richard, ed. *The Pursuit of the Presidency 1980*. New York: Berkley Books, 1980.

Haworth, Paul L. *The Hayes-Tilden Election*. Indianapolis: The Bobbs-Merrill Co., 1927.

Hoyt, Edwin P. *Jumbos and Jackasses*. Garden City, N.Y.: Doubleday, 1960.

Johnson, Gerald W. *Roosevelt: Dictator or Democrat*. New York: Harper & Brothers, 1941.

Josephson, Matthew. *The Politicos, 1865–1896*. New York: Harcourt, Brace and Co., 1938.

Judah, Charles Burnet and George W. Smith. *The Unchosen*. New York: Coward-McCann, 1962.

Kane, Joseph Nathan. *Facts About the Presidents: A Compilation of Biographical and Historical Data*. New York: H.W. Wilson Co., 1981.

Kelly, Frank K. *The Fight for the White House: The Story of 1912*. New York: Crowell, 1961.

Leish, Kenneth W., ed. *The American Heritage Pictorial History of the Presidents of the United States* 2 vols. New York: American Heritage Publishing Co., book trade distribution by Simon and Schuster, 1968.

Lorant, Stefan. *The Glorious Burden: The American Presidency*. New York: Harper and Row, 1968.

Lowe, Jacques. *Portrait: The Emergence of John F. Kennedy.* New York: Bramhall House, 1961.

Lurie, Leonard, *The Running of Richard Nixon.* New York: Coward, McCann and Geoghegan, Inc., 1972.

Mankiewicz, Frank. *Perfectly Clear: Nixon from Whittier to Watergate.* New York: Quadrangle, The New York Times Book Co., 1973.

McCombs, William F. *Making Woodrow Wilson President.* New York: Fairview Publishing Co., 1921.

McCormac, Eugene I. *James K. Polk: A Political Biography.* Berkeley: The University of California Press, 1922.

McCoy, Charles A. *Polk and the Presidency.* Austin: University of Texas Press, 1960.

McCoy, Donald R. *Calvin Coolidge: The Quiet President.* New York: Macmillan and Co., 1967.

McGinniss, Joe. *The Selling of the President 1968.* New York: Trident Press, 1969.

Mencken, H.L. *A Carnival of Buncombe,* ed. Malcolm Moos. Baltimore: The Johns Hopkins Press, 1956.

Merrill, Horace S. *Bourbon Leader: Grover Cleveland and the Democratic Party.* Boston: Little, Brown & Co., 1957.

Miller, Merle. *Plain Speaking: An Oral Biography of Harry S. Truman.* New York: Berkley Publishing Corp., 1973.

Mollenhoff, Clark R. *The Man Who Pardoned Nixon.* New York: St. Martin's Press, 1976.

Moore, Edmund A. *A Catholic Runs for President.* New York: Ronald Press Co., 1956.

Moore, Jonathan and Janet Fraser, eds. *Campaign for President.* Cambridge, MA: Ballinger Publishing Co., 1977.

Moos, Malcolm. *The Republicans: A History of Their Party.* New York: Random House, 1956.

Morgan, James. *Our Presidents.* New York: The Macmillan Co., 1969.

Morison, Samuel Eliot. *The Oxford History of the American People.* New York: Oxford University Press, 1965.

Morrel, Martha McBride. *"Young Hickory." The Life and*

Times of President James K. Polk. New York: E.P. Dutton, 1949.

Moscow, Warren. *Roosevelt and Willkie.* Englewood Cliffs, NJ: Prentice-Hall, Inc., 1968.

Murray, Robert K. *The Harding Era: Warren G. Harding and His Administration.* Minneapolis: University of Minnesota Press, 1969.

Myers, William S. *The Republican Party.* New York: The Century Co., 1931.

O'Donnell, Kenneth P. and David F. Powers. *"Johnny, We Hardly Knew Ye."* New York: Pocket Book, 1973.

Parmet, Herbert S. *Never Again: A President Runs for a Third Term.* New York: Macmillan and Co., 1968.

Paysinger, Mildred A. *You May Quote Me—the Politicians.* Hicksville, NY: Exposition Press, 1974.

Redding, Jack. *Inside the Democratic Party.* Indianapolis: The Bobbs-Merrill Co., Inc., 1958.

Remini, Robert V. *The Election of Andrew Jackson.* Philadelphia: Lippincott, 1963.

Rienow, Robert and Leona Train Rienow. *The Lonely Quest: The Evolution of Presidential Leadership.* Chicago: Follett Publishing Co., 1966.

Rogers, Will. *How We Elect Our Presidents.* Boston: Little, Brown and Co., 1952.

Roseboom, Eugene H. *A History of Presidential Elections.* New York: The Macmillan Co., 1957.

Ross, Irwin, *The Loneliest Campaign: The Truman Victory of 1948.* New York: New American Library, 1968.

Sandberg, Carl. *Abraham Lincoln: The War Years,* 4 vols. New York: Harcourt, Brace and Co., 1939.

Scheer, Robert. "Jimmy Carter: A Candid Conversation with the Democratic Candidate for President." *Playboy,* November 1976, pp. 63–86.

Schlesinger, Arthur M., Jr. *A Thousand Days.* Boston: Houghton Mifflin Co., 1965.

Sellers, Charles. *James K. Polk, Continentalist, 1843–1846*. Princeton, NJ: Princeton University Press, 1957.

Sinclair, Andrew. *The Available Man: The Life Behind the Mask of Warren Gamaliel Harding*. New York: Macmillan and Co., 1965.

Sirica, John J. *To Set the Record Straight*. New York: W.W. Norton and Co., 1979.

Smith, Page. *A New Age Now Begins*, 2 vols. New York: McGraw-Hill Book Co., 1976.

Sorenson, Theodore C. *Kennedy*. New York: Harper and Row, Publishers, 1965.

Stone, Irving. *Clarence Darrow for the Defense*. Garden City, NY: Doubleday and Co., Inc., 1941.

———. *They Also Ran*. New York: Pyramid Books, 1964.

Taylor, John M. *Garfield of Ohio, the Available Man*. New York: W.W. Norton and Co., 1970.

Trager, James. *The People's Chronology: A Year-by-Year Record of Human Events from Prehistory to the Present*. New York: Holt, Rinehart and Winston, 1979.

Truman, Margaret. *Harry S. Truman*. New York: William Morrow and Co., 1973.

Tugwell, Rexford Guy. *How They Became President: Thirty-Five Ways to the White House*. New York: Simon and Schuster, 1968.

Van Deusen, Glyndon G. *Thurlow Weed: Wizard of the Lobby*. Boston: Little, Brown and Co., 1947.

Warren, Sidney. *The Battle for the Presidency*. Philadelphia: J.B. Lippincott Co., 1968.

Weisbord, Marvin R. *Campaigning for President: A New Look at the Road to the White House*. Washington, D.C.: Public Affairs Press, 1964.

White, Theodore H. *Breach of Faith: The Fall of Richard Nixon*. New York: Atheneum Publishers, 1975.

———. *The Making of the President 1960*. New York: Atheneum Publishers, 1961.

_____. *The Making of the President 1964.* New York: Atheneum Publishers, 1965.

_____. *The Making of the President 1968.* New York: Atheneum Publishers, 1969.

_____. *The Making of the President 1972.* New York: Atheneum Publishers, 1973.

Whitney, David C. *The American Presidents.* Garden City, N.Y.: Doubleday and Co., 1975.

Witcover, Jules. *Marathon: The Pursuit of the Presidency 1972–1976.* New York: The Viking Press, 1977.

Zornow, William F. *Lincoln and the Party Divided.* Norman: University of Oklahoma Press, 1954.